Chuck Lawliss

HAWAII

For the Sophisticated Traveler

Photographed by the author

A Wieser & Lawliss Book

McGraw-Hill Book Company

New York   St. Louis   San Francisco   Auckland   Bogotá   Guatemala   Hamburg
Johannesburg   Lisbon   London   Madrid   Mexico   Montreal   New Delhi   Panama
Paris   San Juan   São Paulo   Singapore   Sydney   Tokyo   Toronto

Designed by Allan Mogel

Copyright © 1985 by Chuck Lawliss

ISBN 0-07-036702-7

LIBRARY OF CONGRESS CATALOGING IN PUBLICATION DATA

Lawliss, Chuck.
    Hawaii—for the sophisticated traveler.
      1. Hawaii—Description and travel—1981–   —Guide-
books.   I. Title.
DU622.L37 1985   919.69′044   84-12198
ISBN 0-07-036702-7

Printed in Hong Kong

*This book is dedicated with love to
the people of Hawaii - the Polynesians,
haoles, Japanese, Chinese, Filipinos,
Koreans, Samoans, and the countless
multi-hyphened combinations thereof.
You are a beautiful state's most
beautiful asset.*

CONTENTS

CREDITS AND ACKNOWLEDGMENTS

A special debt of gratitude is owed Margaret Kaufman who contributed greatly to every phase of this project. Lisa Lawliss provided much needed help and support in the last weeks of field work. Special thanks to Jerry Panzo of the Hawaiian Visitors Bureau, Patti Cook of Communications-Pacific, Inc. Transportation was provided through the courtesy of United Air Lines, Aloha Airlines, and Royal Hawaiian Air Service. The hotels and resorts were more than cooperative.

All the photographs were made by the author with three exceptions: Pages 70–71, Don King, Image Bank; Page 117, David Brownell, Image Bank, and Page 176, Bob Abraham.

HONOLULU

GEORGE R ARIYOSHI
GOVERNOR

MESSAGE FROM GOVERNOR GEORGE R. ARIYOSHI

It is a pleasure to extend my aloha to you on the occasion of Hawaii's celebration of 25 years of statehood.

While this silver jubilee represents much in our history, it also recognizes the centuries that preceded statehood, and the creation of a society unique in the nation and the world. To be sure, statehood meant much to these islands. It made us a part of the United States and accorded us the rights and privileges of full citizenship in a country that had accepted our obligations but not totally recognized or accepted our abilities or lifestyles.

While we celebrate 25 years as a participating member of the Union, let us also consider and reflect upon what made this society unique--and continues to do so. First came the Polynesians, braving the dangers and hardships of a voyage across a vast ocean, to volcanic islands that no humans had ever inhabited. These pioneers created a new society and culture, which we still share and benefit from. Then after centuries, a British sea captain came across these islands by chance and life was to be forever altered. There have been many changes in these islands since Captain Cook's arrival 200 years ago, just as there have been many changes elsewhere. But throughout the years and despite enormous changes, the aloha spirit has survived, and fortunately survives today.

Many things went into the granting of statehood for these islands. Included was the history of the Hawaiian people, what they stood for, and the liberty and freedom they fought for. Included was the history of the immigrants who came here from many lands, seeking a better life for themselves and their children, and who contributed through their toil and sacrifices to a better and more understanding society. Certainly included was the citizenship and heroism of our people in the darkest days of World War II. And of the blood our young men spilled on the battlefields of the world as they served an ideal and a cause and their country. Without question, statehood for Hawaii not only was deserved, but had been earned by the sacrifices and the dedication of its people.

But as we look to our heritage, let us also look to our future. We must preserve this national, but very fragile, treasure we call home. We must protect our environment and guide our development with care and prudence. And we must preserve a society in which diversity is a strength rather than a weakness. Let us dedicate ourselves, then, to doing those things which will help our children and future generations to improve upon the legacy of Hawaii and the legacy that statehood represents. Let us also honor those who preceded us and who contributed so significantly to the dignity of all persons. We also give recognition to those who will follow us and continue this society.

The recognition of the worth of everyone is what sets Hawaii apart and truly makes it a very special place.

George R. Ariyoshi

9

"See Naples and die but see Hawaii and live."

Jack London

I first saw Hawaii from the deck of a destroyer. By chance, it was a Thursday morning and the cruise ships were clustered around the Aloha Tower and, as we steamed by, we could hear a band playing *Aloha Oe*. I tingled as only a teenager can. I had been excited about Hawaii since our orders were cut; the days at sea from San Diego were almost unbearably long, especially with the old-timers stoking our enthusiasm with tales of past Hawaiian liberties. The year was 1949. Honolulu was still a small city, Hawaii was still a territory, the Korean War was still a year away, and the Navy was still fun.

My first visit wasn't long and my memory of it reminds me of a broken mirror whose shards catch random reflections; the bus into town, the dubious nightlife of Hotel Street, my gawking at the people on Waikiki Beach, my fascination with a particular tattoo. It never made it to my arm. I had the time, the money, and the courage but never all three at the same time. Lost in that jumble somewhere must be the moment I fell in love with Hawaii, but I can't find it. I do remember that when we left for the Far East I needed no *lei* to throw overboard to tell me if I were coming back.

Now I have visited Hawaii a number of times. One visit was particularly memorable. I flew in one of the first United Air Lines jets to Hawaii on an assignment for that great and lamented magazine, *Holiday*. I stayed at the *Royal Hawaiian*, the queen of the beach, and when I wasn't working I *luxuriated!* I took surfing lessons and cruised at sunset, I went to a *luau* and saw a Polynesian revue—in short, I did everything a first-time tourist usually does and I reveled in it. It was early 1959 and I was only vaguely aware that the countdown to statehood had begun.

In subsequent visits, Hawaii has revealed more and more of itself to me. I have discovered the rest of Oahu and the other islands. I have seen Hawaii's wilderness. I have learned something about the people of Hawaii and their customs and history. Like two lovers exchanging confidences, this has made the bond between Hawaii and myself even stronger.

I have always been a traveler. I love to experience new places, poke around, learn what makes them special. Along the way I have learned that travel involves work and thought. It's much harder to be a traveler than a tourist. A tourist seeks only escape and the pleasure of letting others do things for him, and that's easy to find. Escape is seductive, to be sure, and occasionally it is exactly what one needs. But escape is so fleeting, it fades even faster than a suntan. The rewards of travel are something else again; they last for a lifetime. And the effort that is made to seek out the true pleasures of a place like Hawaii is as personally rewarding as finding them.

This book was written and photographed for travelers like myself. We may not react the same way to the same things, but we do react. We do not rate a place by its ability to provide us with what we left at home. We want the rare, the best, the quintessential, but we reserve the right to make our own judgment about what constitutes the rare, the best, and the quintessential. We respect others' opinions but we have a healthy distrust of conventional wisdom.

This is not a guide book in the usual sense. It blithely ignores a lot about Hawaii that any guide book can tell you. Nor is it a picture book. Always, my intent was to record impressions of specific things, not simply to take pretty pictures. And it most assuredly is not a rich man's guide to Hawaii. There are wealthy tourists, and there are good travelers who must scrimp for a year to take a modest holiday. Some of the things in this book are expensive, to be sure, but in my judgment they are worth the price. Many other things are free or cost about as much as movie tickets.

Finally, here is one person's conception of the best of Hawaii and the information you need to discover it for yourself. If the book is a prelude to your first, or fifth, or fiftieth visit to Hawaii and it helps to increase your enjoyment and understanding, I will be very, very pleased. Great experiences were meant to be shared.

Chuck Lawliss

OAHU

"On no other coast that I know shall you enjoy, in calm, sunny weather, such a spectacle of ocean's greatness, such beauty of changing color, or such degrees of thunder in the sound."
Robert Louis Stevenson

KAHALA HILTON

President Reagan, Nancy, and entourage took a brief holiday here on their way to China. Many of the *Kahala Hilton's* guests would agree it was an impeccable choice. The *Kahala* is on Oahu, which makes it convenient. It is away from the congestion of Waikiki on the other side of Diamond Head, and surrounded on three sides by the *Waialae Country Club.* The secret service must have applauded that. The efficient management is European; the Hawaiian staff, fast and friendly. The setting is glorious, the beach a treasure, and the cuisine, superb. The *Kahala* is accustomed to heads of state dropping by. Queen Elizabeth and Prince Phillip, and Juan Carlos and Queen Sophia spent part of their honeymoon here. Finally, the presidential suite looks like the real thing. For the merely affluent, the *Kahala* is a cornucopia of pleasures. There are 370 rooms in the resort complex, though it feels smaller and more intimate. The main building is handsome, its whiteness complemented by bougainvillea. The light, airy 30-foot-high lobby has a copper sculpture surrounded by orchids, and two huge glass chandeliers. There is a lagoon that is home to two penguins, sea turtles, a variety of rockfish, and four dolphins that put on a lively show for guests at their thrice-daily feedings. A two-story wing overlooks the lagoon, and there are beachside bungalows, both well worth the additional tariff.

On the grounds are more than 50 varieties of flora, including such delights as torch and shell ginger, bird of paradise, Tahitian gardenias, and silver ganzania. A lovely touch: huge searchlights play out on the water at night so the white breakers are clearly visible. The *Maile Restaurant* has an elegant gardenlike atmosphere, and ladies in kimonos serve up such specialties as fresh *mahi-mahi* wrapped in romaine leaves and steamed in white wine, and *opakapapa* baked with fresh vegetables and a dash of Pernod. For breakfast or lunch the open-air *Hala Terrace* has a great ocean view and does wonderful pancakes with coconut syrup. At night on the terrace, the *Danny Kalekini Show* has been a hit since 1967.

Resorts are for relaxing and one young guest takes relaxation to its outer limits, top. The beach bungalows, left, are a pleasant alternative to the main hotel. Dolphins, center above, fly for their supper in the lagoon. A bridge is as likely a place as any for a refreshing drink, above right. The Kahala, opposite above, looks out across the beach to the wide Pacific. Any wonder why there's romance in the air, opposite below? And to think that Waikiki Beach is only a 15-minute drive away.

15

"Waikiki was our heaven always. It was always reserved for the greatest occasions of joy."

Genevieve Taggard

Waikiki, the most famous beach resort in the world, is actually quite small, a mile-and-a-half long and some three-quarters of a mile wide. Into this area have been packed hotels, shopping centers, restaurants, night clubs, lei stands, and you-name-its to degrees that suggests the bursting point is dangerously near. There are more hotel rooms here, some 25,000, than in all the rest of Hawaii put together. In the festivities marking the 25th anniversary of statehood little if any note was made of the coincidence that 1984 also marked the 100th anniversary of the first hotel on Waikiki Beach. It was the *Sans Souci*, long since gone, and one of its early guests was Robert Louis Stevenson, who wrote in the guest book of "pure air, clear sea water, good food, and heavenly sunsets." Those are the attractions of Waikiki today. Mr. Stevenson also mentioned "quiet" as a virtue he found here. That's a little hard to find these days, except by a hotel pool or in one's room. In its place is a 24-hour, seven-day-a-week party that has been going on for years and shows no sign of winding down. The party is fun, the guests obviously are enjoying themselves, but like any party, the trick is not to stay too long. There's too much to see and do in Honolulu, the rest of Oahu, and on the other islands to allow the intoxication of Waikiki to keep you from them.

Seen up close, the frenetic quality of Waikiki Beach dissolves into little vignettes of people relaxing and enjoying the warm sun and clear water. Most are blissfully unaware of everything and everyone around them, but for a confirmed people watcher, a stroll along Waikiki Beach is a fascinating study of a great beach's seduction of the young and old.

18

HALEKULANI

An off-white island of tranquil elegance in the midst of bustling Waikiki, the new *Halekulani* opened late in 1983, replacing a legend. A sea captain's two-story home once stood here on the point where Waikiki Beach begins its graceful sweep toward Diamond Head. It became a small beach hotel in 1907, the Hau Tree Hotel, and was acquired by Clifford Kimball and his wife in 1917. They renamed it *Halekulani*, "house befitting heaven." Natives had called the sea captain's house that out of gratitude for being allowed to keep their canoes under his hau trees. Over the years, the Kimballs improved and expanded the hotel, adding cottages around the property. A new main building replaced the original house in 1931, which has been carefully restored and is the focal point of the new hotel. Nearby is a new open-air lounge, the *House Without a Key*, replacing the original. Author Earl Derr Biggers, a frequent visitor to the old *Halekulani*, introduced Charlie Chan in 1925 in *The House Without a Key*. The *Halekulani* now is the state of the art in elegance: polished marble and terrazo, pure wool carpets, the finest cotton sheets and towels. And the views from the lanais toward Diamond Head are spectacular. Actually comprised of five buildings, ranging from 2 to 16 stories, on five acres, the 456-room hotel gives a remarkable sense of unity. It truly is a "house befitting heaven."

From the main part of the hotel the
new House Without a Key presents a
graceful profile against sea and sky
(opposite). The Presidential Suite, *left*,
is a study in elegance. There are
special robes for guests, and tiny
gift-wrapped seashells are placed on
the pillow each night. Kanoe Miller, a
former Miss Hawaii, dances the hula
each evening at sunset in front of the
century old kiawe tree, a Waikiki
landmark, *left below*. Glistening at
the bottom of the pool, *below*, is a
cattleya orchid, symbol of the hotel.

SHOPPING: SOME HIDDEN TREASURES

To visit Honolulu, especially Waikiki, is to see shops and stores and malls in such profusion that it makes the mind reel. This must be a compulsive shopper's dream of heaven, one muses. A closer inspection suggests that most shops fall into four categories: one, those that offer things to wear on holiday or take home as gifts—T-Shirts, beach paraphernalia, leis, macadamia nuts, *muumuus*, etc.; two, the ubiquitous Liberty House and other stores that mostly cater to the needs of the Hawaiians; three, branches of such international purveyors of luxury items as Gucci, Piaget, and Courréges; and four, the delightful exceptions. These are shops that offer exclusive items that are in their own way a part of the Hawaiian experience. Here are seven such shops that were found after much searching. There are more, of course, but not space here for more. Besides, half the fun is discovering your own.

For women who are beginning to fear that the muu-muu *is the only island attire, a visit to* Mandalay *at the new Halekulani hotel is in order. Here Cynthia Ai, the boutique's manager, and her influential backers (Claire Booth Luce is one) have assembled a collection of authentic Far Eastern clothes. A Mandalay luncheon fashion show is a weekly hit at the hotel. Also featured are a few well-chosen pieces of Oriental art and artifacts. Mandalay has just opened a branch on Maui at Kapula Bay. Cynthia models a smashing evening coat made from an antique kimono, top right, and poses with her staff, all attired in the boutique's fashions. Of special interest are short sleeveless jackets from the Thai hill country. In the background are some fine examples of porcelain.*

The beach boys started it all. Not the singing group but the original Polynesian beach boys who charmed the early visitors to Waikiki, teaching them about surfboards and outriggers, among other things. They all wore colorful, hand-painted shirts, and by the early 1930s, tourists were pestering Chinatown tailors to make similar shirts for them. Ellery J. Chun made the first ready-to-wear beach boy shirt, registering the name Aloha. (Harry Truman loved Aloha shirts: Montgomery Clift wore one in From Here To Eternity.) Modern versions are worn everywhere in the islands, but an old hand-painted one—now called a silkie—is THE shirt to wear. (Look again at Tom Sellek in Magnum P.I. He wears a silkie.) Good ones are hard to find but there's no better collection than at Linda's Vintage Isle. For a vintage silkie in top condition expect to pay from $75 to $100 or more. Above, Linda Sheebon displays two silkies and a vintage muumuu. Patrick Ashbrook, left, shows how elegant a true silkie can be.

23

Those fascinated by military memorabilia should visit the impressive array at The Military Shop of Hawaii, *owned by the Boyers, right. If a soldier, sailor or marine wore it or won it, they probably have it.* The Polynesian art of making intricate feather bands lives on at Nick Reed's Silver Feather. *The hatbands here, below left and right, are things of beauty.*

The gift shop at the Bishop Museum *is an excellent source of gifts for the folks back home. It also stocks a wide selection of books on Hawaiiana, and such exotica as these New Guinea masks, right.*

Windward Oahu is a kite flier's
dream, and Barbara Skaggs and
Robert Loera, above, can make that
dream come true at Kite Fantasy.
There are kites of every description
here, including the prized White Bird
kites. A ganged flight of ten kites, left,
maneuvered by a single kiter,
performs a graceful arabesque against
a background of clouds and
mountains.

To help lead Polynesian maidens in the paths of righteousness, the wives of early missionaries taught them the American craft of quilting. The Polynesians made the craft an art. Striking designs inspired by the flora of the islands were sewn in tens of thousands of delicate stitches. Today Hawaiian quilts are in short supply and a good one will cost several thousand dollars. The best introduction to this art is at Things Hawaiian at the Hyatt Regency Waikiki. Aunty Malia, above, will begin your quilting education and put you in touch with quilters if you wish to buy one. If you are very lucky, you'll see Mama Lake at work here, top, one of the most revered quilters in all the islands.

HYATT REGENCY WAIKIKI

The *Hyatt Regency Waikiki at Hemmeter Center*, to use its full name, is a complex of twin 39-story towers (one is shown, opposite above) linked by a lushly landscaped atrium. The hotel is not on the beach but has easy access to the best part of the beach. What's more important is that it may just be the most *fun* place in Waikiki. The atrium, called the *Great Hall*, has three waterfalls (the photograph below was taken through one of them, another is opposite below), a 34-foot hanging metal sculpture that weighs more than two tons, a pool deck, and a collection of chic shops and restaurants. It is a little world unto itself, and has become *the* "in" place to meet in Waikiki, the equivalent of "under the clock" at New York's old Biltmore. A combination of Dixieland jazz (Have *you* ever heard *Bill Bailey, Won't You Please Come Home?* sung in Japanese?), elegant appointments, free *pupus* (Hawaiian hors d'oeuvres), and a heart-stopping group of waitresses, opposite below, help make *Trapper's* on the lower level *the* bar scene. The genius behind *Trapper's* is an amazing lady, Mai Tai Sing (shown, right, with her artist-uncle Dong Kingman's watercolor of the atrium). She made *The Ricksha* the "in" place in San Francisco and has repeated her success here. *Bagwell's* on the third floor is the equal of any restaurant in the islands. Also of note are *Harry's Bar* by the waterfalls, a swinging disco called *Spats*, and a fine sushi bar in the *Furusato*. Oh yes, there are 1,234 very nice rooms, including some extra special rooms on the *Regency Club* floors.

29

THE ENTERTAINERS

Music is as prevalent as sunshine in Hawaii. It is everywhere. And everyone seems to bring a love of Hawaiian music with them to the islands. As author Jerry Hopkins wrote: "No music has girdled the earth more smoothly, more often and more completely than Hawaiian music and none has remained so popular with so many for so long." Hawaiian music is folk music, each song telling a story. The *hula* is the Hawaiian folk dance, the hands of the dancer also telling a story. What strikes the visitor is the many varieties of Hawaiian music, from ancient chants to traditional songs to very contemporary. Here are some of those who do it best.

At Stouffer's Wailea Beach Hotel, *the Brown Brothers, top, perform traditional Hawaiian music with a lilting softness that is enchanting.* The Danny Kalekini Show *has been a fixture at the Kahala Hilton since 1967 and Danny, center right, still packs them in. Emma Veary, center left, appears at the* Royal Hawaiian Hotel *with the popular* Brothers Cazimero (Robert and Roland, above) *whose music and humor are both contemporary. Opposite, one of the lovely hula dancers at the* Polynesian Cultural Center.

ROYAL HAWAIIAN HOTEL

The Matson Steamship Company built the luxurious *Royal Hawaiian* in 1927 at a cost of $4 million for the passengers on its liners. The "Pink Palace" of Moorish-Spanish design stands on the site of the former summer home of the Kamehameha kings. It played host to both high society and Hollywood stars. Duponts and Rockefellers rubbed elbows with the likes of Douglas Fairbanks and Mary Pickford, Al Jolson and Ruby Keeler. In those days guests came with steamer trunks and servants, and stayed for at least a month. The war ended all that. Honolulu had a strict blackout, there was barbed wire, and soldiers with rifles patroled Waikiki beach. From 1942 to 1947, the *Royal Hawaiian* served as a rest and recreation center for the armed forces, mostly submariners. Reopening, she still dominated the beach until the coming of the Jet Age and Statehood set off the unprecedented Waikiki building boom. Walking along Kalakaua Avenue today you might think the Pink Palace was gone, replaced by the chic *Royal Hawaiian Shopping Center* or the towering *Sheraton Waikiki*. But she is still there, as pink and proud as ever. The grounds are beautiful, the lobby stately, the *Monarch Room* still elegant. For a moment, one feels that things haven't changed much after all.

Some tall neighbors have moved in since the Pink Lady was built in 1927, left above. On the beach guests still have a roped-off area to themselves, right above. Once the cream of society strolled this colonnade, right. The emblem of the Royal Hawaiian, *opposite above, faces the Pacific with pride. The entrance, opposite right, is reached through manicured grounds. The hotel is repainted its traditional pink every five years. A 16-story Royal Tower was added in 1969 but traditionalists prefer one of the 400 rooms in the original building.*

MOANA HOTEL

The oldest hotel on Waikiki Beach is the *Moana* and when it was built in 1901 at a cost of $150,000 it was *the* hotel in the islands. (The Prince of Wales stayed here on his round-the-world tour.) It boasted private baths for each of its 75 rooms and private telephones. New wings were added in 1918, the old *Surfrider* was incorporated into it and renamed the *Ocean Lanai Wing*, bringing the room total to 390. The nostalgic should request one of the 130 restored rooms in the original hotel; brass beds, marble-top night tables, and ceiling paddle fans in lieu of air-conditioning. A huge banyan tree behind the *Moana* shades the best beach bar on Waikiki. In the late 1900s, Robert Louis Stevenson did some of his writing under its spreading branches. The trunk is 40 feet in circumference, the branches 140.

THE RESTAURANTS

One of the pleasures of Waikiki is the number of fine restaurants nearby and the wide variety of dining experiences they offer. Not to try at least some of them during your holiday would be a major blunder. Some of the best restaurants are discussed in the pages devoted to individual hotels—the *Maile* at the *Kahala Hilton*, *Bagwell's* at the *Hyatt Regency*, *La Mer* at the *Halekulani*, the *Monarch Room* at the *Royal Hawaiian*, *Champeaux's* at the *Westin Ilikai*—and all are worthy of a visit. Others of note include *The Willows*, opposite, owned and managed by Randy Lee, formerly general manager of the old *Halekulani*. Dispel any notion that in a place that looks this good the food must suffer. It doesn't. This is the best spot in Honolulu to sample the traditional Hawaiian poi supper—or rack of lamb or Chinese wok cooking, for that matter. In the *Kamaaiana Suite* on the second-floor overlooking the carp pond is a gourmet's paradise; both the nouvelle cuisine and the curries are superb. For authentic Thai food *Keo's*, below left, is unmatched. Some like it hot and they should try the Evil Jungle Prince (a blend of chicken, melon grass, coconut milk, fish sauce, Chinese cabbage, red chilis and fresh Thai leaves). *Yen King*, below right, serves the cuisine of North China with skill and panache. *Michel's* at the *Colony Surf* offers a combination of continental dishes, dining with a magnificent view of the beach, and superlative service. A weekday brunch here is a special treat. Not to be confused with *Michel's* is *Chez Michel*, perhaps the finest French restaurant in town. *Restaurant Suntory* is the best bet for elegant Japanese dining; the sushi bar here is what all sushi bars should aspire to be. The *Third Floor* at the *Hawaiian Regent Hotel* is a perennial contender for top honors and it's perhaps the most beautiful dining experience in Honolulu. Dinner begins with an unusual treat: hot Indian *naan* breast with goose-liver pate. The *Bistro Diamond Head* is *tres chic* and ideal for a late supper. The wine list is both good and reasonable. For seafood lovers *John Dominis* is a handsome and impeccable choice. *King Tsin* is an ordinary-looking restaurant that does extraordinary Szechuan cooking. One dining experience is a nuisance to arrange but well worth the effort. At the *Nuuanu Onsen*, a Japanese tea house in the Manoa Valley, one must reserve at least 24 hours in advance, have a party of six or more, choose what each person will eat when the reservation is made, and pay ten percent of the tab in advance. For this expect an unforgettable meal, perfect service, and a post-prandial introduction to Japanese parlor games. And for a fast snack pull into any one of the many *Zippy's* for saimin, tempura or chili. *Zippy's* are a creative Hawaiian approach to fast food and a welcome change from their mainland counterparts.

WESTIN ILIKAI

Tennis players and yachtsmen have a natural affinity for this 30-floor, 800-room hotel on the western (city) end of Waikiki. Its seven courts and able staff of pros comprise the only tennis complex on the beach. A few steps away is the marina where most of the big sail on Oahu ties up. The open area at lobby level has a swimming pool, fountains and terraces, a popular meeting place, particularly at sundown when a Hawaiian trio performs. Rooms at the *Westin Ilikai* are comfortable, well furnished and spacious, more like large studio apartments than hotel rooms. One of the best restaurants in the area has a stunning 30th-floor view: *Champeaux's*. The specialties of Chef Harrison Ramey include lychee flambée, warm duck salad, and strawberries Renaissance.

A glass elevator, top, presents a beautiful panorama of the Pacific as it whisks passengers to Champeaux's *or* Annabelle's. *Tennis facilities here are tops, center. The yacht basin, below; at sunset, painted by the* Southern Cross, *opposite..*

HONOLULU OLD AND NEW

"It is a meeting place of East and West: The very new rubs shoulders with the immeasurably old," wrote W. Somerset Maugham in his book *Honolulu*. He meant the peoples and cultures of the city, but his observation applies as well to the city's architecture. In the last two decades Honolulu has grown tremendously, becoming a city in the true sense. Someone seeing it for the first time since the war would shake his head in wonder, hard put to match his memories with the new realities. A few landmarks remain: the Aloha Tower, the Palace area, Chinatown, the Royal Hawaiian. A sky-line of tall buildings now competes with Diamond Head as the city's most memorable sight. Much of the new is excellent, as fine a demonstration of modern architecture as to be found anywhere. Yet much of the warp and woof of the old city remains, rubbing shoulders, as Mr. Maugham pointed out, with the new, and with a comfortable charm that is beguiling. In the center photograph just below, note how easily the Dillingham Transportation Building sits with its new neighbors; how the old facades, opposite, add a grace note to an office tower. In this beautiful state, it is easy to overlook the fact that Honolulu is one of the most beautiful cities in all the U.S.

38

THE IOLANI PALACE

The only royal palace in the United Sates was dedicated in 1888 during the reign of King David Kalakaua known as the *Merry Monarch*. He loved the good life, particularly the trappings of European royalty. He and his wife, Queen Kapiolani, entertained lavishly. King Kalakaua died in 1891, the *Iolani Palace* his greatest legacy. His successor, Queen Liliuokalani, lost her throne in a 1891 coup and royalty in Hawaii ended. Until 1969, when the new state capitol was built, the palace was used as the seat of government: the House of Representatives met in the throne room, the Senate in the royal dining room. During this period, the palace fell into disrepair, and most of its original furnishings were sold. The non-profit *Friends of Iolani Palace* was formed in 1969 to restore the palace. It has raised 9 million dollars and the palace (which cost $360,000 to build a century ago) is in magnificent shape. The Friends now are painstakingly locating and retrieving as many of the original furnishings as possible. They also conduct tours of the palace. The throne room, the royal dining room, and some bedrooms are furnished.

A century ago the entrance to Iolani Palace, *opposite, used to welcome European royalty and other visiting dignitaries. Inside the palace, the royal crest graces a quilted bedspread, top left. The grand staircase, top center, is an outstanding example of craftsmanship. The sweeping porch, top right, the Corinthian columns and the tall, shuttered windows combine classic and island-inspired architecture. From across the street, the famous statue of King Kamehameha, above right, seems to point out the palace to the visitor. It was Kamehameha who conquered the islands of Hawaii and united them under his rule. The Hawaiian state seal appears on the palace gate, above left, and on an etched glass window in the palace. The state's motto, at the bottom, translated from the Hawaiian is:* The life of the land is perpetuated in righteousness.

Across from the Palace is the governor's mansion, Washington Place, top, once the home of Queen Liliuokalani. Since 1969, the legislature, right, has met in the new Capitol, which is open to the sky, above. Opposite is King Lunalilo's Tomb on the grounds of Kawaiahao Church. He is the only Hawaiian monarch not buried in the Royal Mausoleum in Nuuanu Valley, requesting on his death bed to be buried closer to his people.

ROYAL HAWAIIAN BAND

One of the pure delights of the Palace area is the free Friday noon concert of the *Royal Hawaiian Band*. The band plays in the gazebo-like, gaily painted *Coronation Stand* built in 1883 for King Kalakaua and Queen Kapiolani's grand coronation ceremony. The band dates from the days of King Kamehameha V who decided he wanted a royal band, and imported a German bandmaster to head it up. He was Heinrich Berger, known today as the Father of Hawaiian music. Serving as director from 1872 to 1915, he arranged more than a thousand Hawaiian songs, composed 75 Hawaiian songs himself, and trained two generations of Hawaiian musicians. Today the band is led by bandmaster Aaron David Mahi, opposite left, the numbers are introduced by George Hookane, opposite middle, who recently retired after more than 50 years as a band member. The vocalist is Nalani Olds, opposite right. A traditional part of the concert is the hula, above right. People come with box lunches to enjoy the concert under tall trees. Hula, opposite top, is part of every concert.

"My grandfather told me that when the first missionaries came, the islands emptied into the sea to greet them. Mothers swam with babies, and the old people were taken to the ships in outriggers. My grandfather told me the people covered the missionaries with so many flowers you could barely see their faces. When the missionaries came ashore with their children, they were like new brothers and sisters. All of them, without exception. My grandfather said the people of the islands treated the missionaries like a great big wonderful prize that had come out of the ocean. But the missionaries weren't happy. They saw too much evil in these smiling islands. All that naked skin. All that laughter. All that eating and singing and chasing around. The missionaries had to remove the evil. First they took away our gods and substituted their gods, then they took away our land. They took away our queen and our palace. They made us dress like them and act like them. But they won't let us *be* like them. Or be *with* them, except to work in their fields or in their kitchens. They have ruined us. We were a free and easy people on these islands who didn't know any other way except to love. They outlawed love. The missionaries' sons brought the guns and the police, and the Navy did the rest."

Princess Luahine

A hula dancer, Waimea Falls Park, th
Mission Houses Museum.

QUEEN EMMA'S SUMMER PALACE

In the *Nuuanu Valley* above Honolulu is the summer palace of Queen Emma, wife of Kamehameha IV. It was built between 1847 and 1850 and first owned by John Young, Queen Emma's uncle and son of the chief British adviser to the king. The royal couple bought it and named it *Hanaiakamalama*, Foster Child of the Moon, after a Polynesian demigoddess. The family used this house as a cool retreat. In 1857, a large back room was added in anticipation of a visit by the Duke of Edinburgh, Queen Victoria's second son. He never came but the room still is called the Edinburgh Room. After Queen Emma's death in 1885, the house fell into disrepair. About to be torn down in 1913, it was saved by the Daughters of Hawaii. The society restored the palace and has operated it as a museum since 1915. It is beautifully furnished and contains some fascinating artifacts: an elaborate Gothic cabinet, a gift from Prince Albert, Queen Victoria's consort; a stereopticon, a gift from Napoleon III, and the christening robe of Queen Emma's only son, Albert, who died here at the age of four. Kamehameha IV and Queen Emma joined the Anglican church and their political and personal financial support was instrumental in building St. Andrew's Cathedral. The royal couple were regular and devout communicants here. It now is the seat of the Espiscopalian bishop, opposite.

The palace, top, is unpretentious, looking more like the house of a prosperous businessman. The royal crib, above left, of Queen Emma's only son, Albert. The queen's bedchamber, right. Behind the bed are tall feather kahili, *royal standards used for meditation and at funerals. Queen Emma said they symbolized that "life is often flying on another plane, stripped of its body."*

ON THE WATERFRONT

A century ago, this four-masted square rigger made the run from San Francisco to Hilo on the Big Island. Now restored and under the wing of the Bishop Museum, she is a thing of beauty. Her stern, opposite, and toprigging, left, speak of an era sadly past. Below are her figurehead, brass builder's plate, and the sweetheart of a long forgotten sailor. The Falls of Clyde is the last of her kind in the world. The Oceania, center left, was built in Hong Kong and towed to Honolulu. A dragon, below, guards the gangway which leads to shops and several Chinese restaurants.

SS CONSTITUTION AND INDEPENDENCE

Should you take a cruise or a holiday in Hawaii? Do both! Two lovely sister ships, the *Constitution* and the *Independence*, operated by American Hawaii Cruises, board passengers every Saturday near the Aloha Tower and sail just after dark. The *Constitution* cruises by Molokai, Lanai, and docks at Hilo and Kona on the Big Island, at Kahului on Maui, and Nawiliwili on Kauai, arriving back at Honolulu on Saturday morning. The *Independence* makes the same voyage in reverse order. While in port the ships are floating hotels. Passengers have a choice of packaged shore trips or renting a car to explore on their own. There is a car rental desk on board at each port of call and cars are parked at the gangway. Both vessels are in A-one condition with excellent cuisine and all the usual diversions of cruise ships at hand.

BISHOP MUSEUM

This is Hawaii's Smithsonian, the repository of its past, its attic. Founded in 1889 by Charles Reed Bishop, it honors the Hawaiian heritage of his wife, Princess Pauahi. On three levels, it traces the islands from prehistoric times until now. The first level, *The Legacy of the Past*, has artifacts that pre-date the arrival of Captain Cook. The second level, *Conflict and Consonance*, shows the Western influence on islanders. The third level, *Living in Harmony*, displays materials from other parts of Polynesia. *A Science Center, Hall of Natural History, planetarium, Garden Courtyard,* and special exhibits in the *Kahili Room* round out this magnificent presentation. The Bishop Museum is a must for anyone seriously interested in Hawaii.

The gray stone fortress, above, has the greatest collection of Hawaiian cultural and natural history specimens in the world. A 55-foot, 22-ton sperm whale dominates the interior of the museum. A London double-decker bus links the Bishop with the Falls of Clyde *and King's Alley in Waikiki. A ticket to the museum or the ship allows a free ride between the two.*

A restoration of King Kalakaua's crown. Pillaged in 1893, it was forgotten until 1925 when $350 was appropriated to have it restored with synthetic materials.

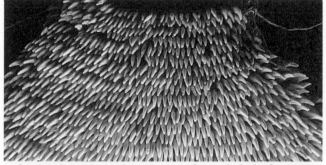

A dog-tooth ankle rattle once worn by male hula dancers. Each anklet consisted of a thousand or so teeth, taking the incisors of 250 dogs to equip one dancer.

This feather cloak, one of the largest known, was collected in 1789, during the voyage of the Columbia Rediviva, *the first American ship to circumnavigate the globe.*

Detail of a formal dress uniform favored by the monarchy during the late 19th Century. Inspired by the British court attire, the design incorporated taro and fern leaves.

A feathered covered basketry image constructed of split roots, human hair, mother-of-pearl, netting, and feathers. The eyes are wooden pegs; the teeth are dog's teeth.

A cotton quilt with a representation of the Hawaiian royal coat of arms. The legend Kuuhae Hawaii *means "My Beloved Flag." Quilts like this were used by royalty.*

A reproduction of the largest stone image, or ahu, *found on Easter Island, which was destroyed in the 1960 tidal wave. This one stands nine feet high and weighs six tons.*

JOHN GUILD INN

And now for something entirely different. In the lovely and fashionable *Monoa Valley* area near the University of Hawaii campus, a mansion has been restored, furnished with antiques and made a most elegant "bed and breakfast," the first of its kind in Hawaii. In 1919, John Guild, a director of Alexander & Baldwin, one of Hawaii's "Big Five" corporations, bought a modest house on this site and converted it into a mansion. Mr. Guild achieved some notoriety in 1922 when he was jailed for embezzling $775,000 from his company. The house fell on hard times in recent years and was used as a student rooming house. The building was scheduled for demolition in 1978, when it was bought by Rick Ralston, founder of Hawaii's ubiquitous *Crazy Shirts*, and an avid antique collector. The mansion, now on the National Register of Historic Places, debuted as the *John Guild Inn* on Valentine's Day, 1984. There are six bedrooms, a suite and a small cottage. The bedrooms share baths. Guests are served fruit, juice, pastry and coffee or tea in the morning, wine and fruit and cheese in the afternoon. Peter Johnson, who owns a similarly restored inn in Newport, Rhode Island, is the capable manager.

A 1920s mansion today, top left, John Guild once could see Waikiki Beach through the veranda doors, but now there is a view of the city's skyline, opposite below. Each bedroom is furnished differently, but in correct period style, left, and named after someone important in Hawaii's business history. The exception: the (Frances) Beaumont Room was named after the silent movie star and nearly all its furnishings were hers. The charm of the inn can be seen in the first floor sitting room, above. Around the inn are a pump reed organ, an upright piano, a wind-up phonograph and a nickelodeon (the ancestor of the jukebox)—all in working order.

THE SOLEMN PRIDE
THAT MUST BE YOURS
★★ TO HAVE LAID ★★

ERNEST·TAYLOR·PYLE
INDIANA
SC3 USNRF
WORLD WAR I
AUG 3 1900   APRIL 18 1945

D 109

EDWARD
MASAUS
VIETNAM
ARMY
KAKAZU
JAN V 1946
NOV 8 1983

PUNCHBOWL

The ancient Hawaiians called this extinct volcano Puowaina *or* Hill of Sacrifice, *an appropriate site for the* National Memorial Cemetery of the Pacific, *the final resting place for some 26,000 men and women of World War I and II, the Korean and Viet Nam wars, and their dependents. Punchbowl is dominated by a large memorial at one end, opposite. The dead lie beneath plain tablets in neat rows, left. Correspondent Ernie Pyle, who immortalized his friends, the GIs, is the one civilian buried here, above. Among the dead are 22 recipients of the Congressional Medal of Honor. On marble walls in the Court of the Missing are more than 26,000 names of servicemen missing in action. Punchbowl,* top, *is ethereal in dawn's early light. On Easter morn thousands attend a special service. The cemetery is one of Hawaii's most visited places.*

HOTEL STREET

Years ago, Hotel Street was where sailors from Pearl and soldiers from Schofield came for booze and bimbos. (Remember *From Here to Eternity?* Montgomery Clift met Donna Reed working in a joint here; Frank Sinatra fought Fatso in an alley off Hotel Street.) It's still here, sleazier than ever. The only changes are the topless-bottomless shows and the openness with which they are promoted. But that's the permissiveness of the times, not Hotel Street's decadence. It is a curiosity to be seen on an afternoon stroll through Chinatown, which it borders, but dangerous at night.

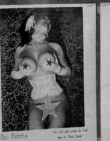

CULTURAL CENTER

*Sun Yat-sen, Father of Modern China,
above, keeps an eye on the new
Cultural Center, a handsome array of
temples, top, interesting shops, and
various services to the Chinese
community. At a nearby skateboard
rink a boy and his shadow explore the
thrill of the sport.*

PEARL HARBOR

The war came to America a few minutes before eight in the morning, Sunday, December 7, 1941, when 360 planes from a Japanese carrier task force 150 miles to the north dropped below cloud cover and attacked every major military installation on Oahu. Pearl Harbor, home of the U.S. Pacific Fleet, was hardest hit. Lost or severely damaged were eight battleships, three light cruisers, three destroyers and four miscellaneous vessels. (By a lucky accident, the U.S. carriers were at sea.) By comparison, Japan lost four midget submarines. The United States suffered 3,435 military and naval losses. Japan, less than 100. A board of inquiry later termed the attack "the greatest military and naval disaster in our nation's history." Pearl Harbor is still the home of the Pacific fleet. (The giant carrier *Kitty Hawk* was photographed from the Visitor's Center.) Visitors come, though, not to see modern warships but to be ferried to what was known as Battleship Row. There a graceful white concrete structure straddles the sunken hull of the U.S. Arizona and the remains of the 1,001 sailors who went down with her when she exploded and sank. Commercial tour boats sail by the Arizona Memorial but only those who take the Navy tour are allowed aboard. It is a powerfully moving experience and worth the effort. There is a museum at the visitor's center where a 20-minute film brilliantly sets the stage for the boat trip to the memorial.

Visitors at the Arizona Memorial, above right, can see the hull of the battleship, above left, and the rusting remains of the ship's Number One gun turret, below. An impressive sight in the memorial is a marble tablet inscribed with the names of those who died aboard. A smiling guide, right, helps keep things running smoothly at Hawaii's most popular attraction.

WAIMEA FALLS

One hour from Waikiki is *Waimea Falls*, one of the loveliest island parks. The falls are small but the tropical gardens are a walk through a paradise of trees, shrubs, and plants brought here from other parts of the world. Exotic birds are everywhere; peacocks, the rare *nene* geese (the state bird), and Kona nightingales. The traditional Hawaiian hula is performed in a meadow — quite different from what is usually seen in Polynesian revues. The old Hawaiian game of *ulu maika*, a form of lawn bowling, is taught nearby. There are trams with guides who identify the more unusual specimens in the gardens.

A bird thinks things over on a lily pad, opposite top. The falls are a popular swimming and sunbathing spot, opposite below. A championship diver climbs to a ledge by the falls, above left, and executes a perfect swan dive, above center. She is joined by another champion diver in a double dive, above right.

SHERATON MAKAHA RESORT AND COUNTRY CLUB

Great golf and the convenience of Oahu come in only one package, and a beautiful one it is — the *Sheraton Makaha Resort and Country Club*, a 30-minute drive from the airport. It's a bit cooler here than at the beach and absolutely lovely. Several clusters of attractive two-story cottages house the 200 guest rooms, each with a private lanai overlooking the course or back to the Pacific. The poolside *Patio* is an ideal breakfast spot before teeing off. And the *Kaala Room* (dinner only) has an excellent continental menu. Between times the *West Course*, a William P. Bell design, 7,252-yarder with 70 sand traps and nine water hazards, beckons. Most say that the fifth hole is the most difficult, a 460-yard par four with a tough dog-leg right to a small trapped green. Watch out for the ninth, though. It takes a well-placed 147-yard tee shot over water to reach the center of a well-bunkered, undulating green. Guests also may play the *Makaha Valley East Course*, a few steps away but separately owned. It is shorter (6,197 yards), hillier, less challenging, with much lower green fees. For beachlovers the hotel provides a shuttle service to Makaha Beach (home of the annual Makaha International Surfing Championships) where it has changing facilities, rest rooms, backrests and towels. Back at the hotel there are four lighted tennis courts, an equestrian center, a one-mile physical fitness course, bicycle rentals and a mini-playground. For those hankering after night life there's a shuttle to Waikiki.

The *Makaha Valley* is rich in history. Scientists believe it was settled in the 13th Century when, as was the custom, the chiefs of the *ali'i nui* were apportioned an *ahupua'a*, a section of land stretching from the mountains to the sea. Each *ahupua'a* was self-sufficient with enough fishing waters and fertile land to support its population. After the decline of the old Hawaiian feudal society, this valley had numerous owners. It once belonged to Governor Boki and his wife, Liliha. They ceded the valley to Chief Paki who later sold it to a group of Scottish and English ranchers, the Holt clan. Until its purchase in 1946 by financier Chinn Ho, the valley was first a cattle ranch, a coffee plantation, a rice plantation and a sugar plantation. The *Kaneaki Heiau*, a restored ancient Hawaiian temple, is nearby and the remains of old plantation structures still dot the valley.

For an experience to treasure drive to Dillingham Field in Nokulei on the North Shore and go gliding with the *Honolulu Soaring Club, Inc.* Swoop over the surf at Sunset Beach; startle cattle on the cliffs above the field. The winds and updrafts of Oahu are perfect for soaring. Many island airline pilots soar here on their days off for the pure joy of it. Or have Bill Johns of the *Puka Air Company*, opposite above right, take you around the island in his small plane. He'll point out all the sights, including Kolekole Pass through which Japanese planes roared on their way to bomb Schofield Barracks and Pearl Harbor that long-ago Sunday morning.

"I could not help concluding that this man felt the most supreme pleasure while he was driven so fast and so smoothly by the sea."

Captain James Cook
Log entry, December 1778

The first Western observers of the Polynesian sport of surfing were Captain Cook and his crew. Surfing is fascinating to watch and before too long *haoles* were trying it for themselves. Samuel Clemens noted: "I tried surf bathing once... but made a failure of it. I got the board placed right, at the right moment, too, but missed the connection myself. The board struck the shore in three-quarters of a second, without any cargo, and I struck the bottom about the same time, with a couple of barrels of water in me." The sport of Hawaiian royalty quickly caught on. In 1912 champion surfer Duke Hahanamoku gave a demonstration at Atlantic City and later in Australia. The Duke, however, rode a 100-pound board, not something anyone can handle. Lightweight boards were developed after World War II and changed all that. Now there is a range of board sizes for the beginner to the professional. The pros compete late in the year on the North Shore when the world's most famous waves, shown here, are at their height. Riding "elephant guns," boards that range up to 20 feet in length, they converge at *Waimea Bay*, *Sunset Beach* and *Banzai Beach*, where shooting through the tunnel formed by the curl of a giant wave — called the *Banzai Pipeline* — is the ultimate surfing challenge.

POLYNESIAN CULTURAL CENTER

On Brigham Young University's Hawaiian campus at Laie on Oahu's windward coast is a 42-acre complex that contains seven architecturally accurate replicas of ancient South Sea island villages. Hawaii, Tonga, Fiji, Samoa, Tahiti, the Marquesas, and New Zealand are represented. Students with appropriate ethnic backgrounds work here, explaining to visitors the life, customs, crafts, ceremonies, and foods of their homelands. Tonga women make tapa cloth, Hawaiians make poi. Tahitians make shell *leis*. Both the similarities and the differences in the cultures are fascinating and revealing. There are three shows a day: a welcoming show in the morning that is a mixture of authentic song and dance and contemporary show business, the afternoon Pageant of the Long Canoes up the lagoon, and the evening extravaganza which pulls out all stops to entertain. A major tourist attraction on the island, it is well worth a visit for the villages, the boat ride, and the enthusiasm and good humor of the students. The shows have a Disneyesque quality to them, so let your opinion of Mr. Disney's work be your guide. Allow a day even if you're not staying for the evening performance.

Visitors at the center may travel from native village to village in a double-hulled canoe poled by a Brigham Young University Hawaii student who uses this unique way to help pay for his education, top. This native ceremonial hut, right, is representative of the Marquesas, an island group some 800 miles north of Tahiti. (There the greeting word is Kaoha (kah-OH-hah) not Aloha, as it is in Hawaii.) Two visitors prepare to have their photograph taken in native costume, opposite top, as a matched pair of friends look on. At the morning Aloha Festival, a spear bearer and a hula dancer, opposite left and right, welcome visitors with smiles and high spirits. By compressing Oceania into a living museum, the Polynesian Cultural Center shows how thousands of years ago a people shared a common heritage that is still evidenced in the similarities of their languages and traditions. The differences came when they sailed to settle on desolate islands spread over a 16-million-square-mile area.

BYODO-IN TEMPLE

Near Kanohe on the Windward Side in the *Valley of the Temples Memorial Park* is a replica of the 900-year-old *Byodo-In Temple* in Kyoto, Japan, majestically sited below the *Koolau* Mountains, opposite. Built in 1968 to honor Hawaii's first Japanese immigrants, it has a three-ton bronze bell one can ring and an 18-foot-high Buddha. Unlike the original, this temple is made of concrete not wood.

On the temple grounds is a 2-acre reflecting pond where swans, ducks, and some 10,000 carp (*koi*) of a myriad of color combinations delight visitors with their voracious appetites and round, gaping mouths, left and below. Carp, which can live over a hundred years, are considered in Japan to symbolize good luck. More than one out of four Hawaiians are of Japanese descent and only the mainland U.S. sends more visitors to Hawaii than Japan.

Mountains in the clouds, top, and a coastline of ever-changing beauty, below, distinguish the eastern side of Oahu. For the hearty there is a hiking trail to the summit of Diamond Head, offering vistas of Waikiki Beach and the city beyond, and the lighthouse at the point of the island, opposite.

KAUAI

"Most beautiful, most blessed Kauai. Serene she rests, rising from the sea to lift the leaf-bud of her mountain Waialeale to the sky—"

Ancient Hawaiian Chant

COCO PALMS RESORT HOTEL

Coco Palms and Grace Guslander are one and indivisible. Since becoming general manager in 1954, she has made it her vision of what an island resort hotel should be. Every evening of the year, she hosts an early evening cocktail party for her guests, then as darkness falls, drums beat and a conch shell blows, right. And as native-dressed youths run along the lagoon lighting dozens of torches, Grace dramatically recites the story of the ceremony. Guests return to the *Coco Palms* year after year, and every guest, old or new, is proud to be a friend of Grace's. Across the lagoon from the three-story, 416-room hotel is a grove of some 2,000 century-old palm trees. Among the palms are scattered thatched-roof honeymoon cottages. The *Coconut Palace Restaurant*, arguably the best on the island, offers a pleasing melange of American-Chinese-Polynesian dishes. Another choice, the *Lagoon Dining Room*, is the best place to see the torch lighting ceremony. There are three restful pools, below, and a plethora of activities: tennis, croquet, fishing in the lagoon, billiards, even a small zoo. Besides *Blue Hawaii*, *Sadie Thompson* was filmed here as well as parts of *Fantasy Island*. Movie buffs will have a distinct feeling of *déjà vu* at the *Coco Palms*.

80

It was by this lovely lagoon, top, that Elvis Presley was married in Blue Hawaii. A Coco Palms postcard commemorates the noteworthy occasion. The small chapel on the resort grounds, left, is the scene of many real weddings. Coming to Hawaii to get married, combining the service and honeymoon, as it were, is becoming increasingly popular. A small building near the chapel houses the resort's museum and library, which has a most impressive collection of first editions of books about the island. The curator, Sarah Sheldon, above, is equally impressive. A font of information about the collection, she is also a superb quilter who can point guests to great bargains in Hawaiian quilts and pillows.

GROVE FARM HOMESTEAD

George Wilcox was the brilliant and ambitious son of a missionary. As a teenager he spent eight months collecting bat guano on a lonely atoll to sell as fertilizer to finance his engineering education at Yale. Returning from college, he devised a plan to irrigate the arid land near *Nawiliwili Bay* with the water that runs off the mountains. Water is the key to growing sugar cane; it takes a ton of water to make a pound of sugar. The soil in the islands is rich in lime, potash, phosphoric acid, and nitrogen, and with enough water Hawaiian fields yield the richest sugar crops in the world. With his dream and his persuasiveness, he purchased the original acreage in 1864 for no money down. He was 25 years old. His irrigation system worked. He rigged a rain gauge on the homestead so he would know how much water to pipe in and when. For the arduous stoop labor in the fields, he brought in Chinese who lived in barracks and worked from sunup to sundown six days a week. Part of their meager wages were withheld to be paid them at the end of their work contract. When that time came, to a man they took the money and ran to an easier and more lucrative life in Honolulu. To stabilize his work force, Wilcox hit on the idea of building cottages and letting his workers bring in wives from China. Soon a bride-by-mail business was thriving. In later years, field workers also were brought in from Japan and the Philippines. Grove Farm grew and prospered for nearly 75 years and, after the company headquarters moved, was a self-sufficient family estate for 40 more. Mabel Wilcox, a niece of the founder and the last of the line, decided Grove Farm should be a museum. Two years after her death in 1976 it was opened to the public. To visit Grove Farm today is to go back in time. Everything in the compound has been carefully restored. The grounds abound with pines, ironwoods, palms, and various varieties of fruit trees. Most of the furniture in the impressive main house was made by native craftsmen from *koa* wood. George Wilcox's office looks as if he might step through the door and pick up where he left off. In fact, one has the feeling not of visiting a museum but rather of being shown around a working homestead when the family and workers were away for a few days. The guides are excellent, full of interesting history and tidbits of gossip.

A silver comb, brush and mirror, above left, are a gentle reminder of the prosperity of the sugar plantation. A charming guide in a traditional muumuu, *above center, tells of a way of life that once flourished here. The tedium of running a big plantation was relieved by a steady flow of business and social guests who were quartered in the guest house, above right. Workers and their families lived in cottages near the fields, opposite above. The children of workers were educated with but not allowed to play with the children of the big house. One glance at the woodshed, opposite below, tells of the Wilcox New England heritage. A special treat for guests now is mint tea and macadamia nut cookies in the old kitchen served by a Japanese lady who cooked for the family for 40 years.*

SHERATON COCONUT BEACH HOTEL

There are a number of excellent hotels along
Wailua Beach, but none nicer than the *Sheraton
Coconut Beach*, a 311-room, multi-winged modern building that is beautifully situated in nearly
11 acres of coconut palms on an excellent part of
the beach. All rooms have small *lanais*, most with
ocean views. A note of caution: swimming on
Wailua Beach is good when the waves are small
but big surf brings strong, dangerous currents.
The main dining room, the *Voyage Room*, is comfortable and open-air, facing the beach and
ocean. Try the shrimp breaded with coconut,
deep fried and served with papaya chutney. You
might finish with the *Plantation Coupe*, sliced
Hawaiian bananas and macadamia nuts cooked in
spices and liqueurs, and served over vanilla ice
cream. The *Coconut Beach* also has an excellent
luau four nights a week in a grove of palm trees
once the haunt of Hawaiian royalty. Entertaining
Bill Lemm explains the *imu* ceremony, and the
feast is first-rate, as is Victor and Kuulei Punua's
Polynesian show. The *Coconut Beach* is near the
Coconut Plantation Market Place, chock-a-block
full of interesting shops and cute restaurants. The
Bull Shed is a good bet if you crave a prime rib.

The public areas at Coconut Beach *are light and airy,
opposite. Balconies on each floor look down on the lobby.
To the right of the stained glass window, a 40-foot
waterfall cascades into a reflecting pool. A windsurfer,
right, takes off from Wailua Beach. The lobby
tapestry, right above, captures the mood and colors of the
South Seas. Look at the picture, above, sip a Mai Tai, hum
Lovely Hula Hands, imagine the aroma of an* imu *roasted
pig, and you will have captured the feel of the Coconut
Beach's popular* luau.

WAIOLI MISSION HOUSE

What was life like for the early missionaries in Hawaii? A good way to find out is to visit the *Waioli Mission House* in *Hanalei.* It is a charming, two-storied house, above right and opposite, looking much more like New England than Kauai. Most of the house actually was built on the mainland and shipped here in prefabricated sections, a surprisingly modern project for that era. It is completely furnished with period pieces and artifacts, some American and some made by the family or local craftsmen. The missionary life may have been a lonely one, and the problems of educating the natives and tending to their spiritual needs immense, but the house certainly was comfortable and the setting magnificent. A brief chronology helps round out the story. In 1834, Rev. William P. Alexander, his wife and small son, came from Wiamea by double canoe and settled into a new grass house. In a year they had organized the Waioli church and some thousand natives were attending services. A school also was functioning. In 1837, the present house was finished, and Edward and Lois Johnson came as teachers. In 1841, a new church of thatch and plaster was built. Seven acres of sugar cane was sold to help pay for the church, bell, and school. The parish continued to grow and prosper until 1863, when the mission lost its American support and the mission lands were divided among the remaining missionaries. The house was restored in 1921 along with the old church nearby, and since has been open to the public as a museum.

WAIOHAI HOTEL

Once upon a time, the *Waiohai* was 47 cottages on a beautiful beach. Now it is a $60-million, 21-suite luxury hotel on a beautiful beach, the showcase of the Amfac chain, and the poshest hotel in Kauai. From the air, the hotel, set in 11 acres of landscaped gardens, resembles a giant letter W, pointing to the beach. This configuration permits all the rooms to have at least a partial view of the ocean. Two of *Waiohai's* advantages are the weather and the beach. This is the sunniest and driest part of the island; the beach is unsurpassed for swimming and snorkeling. Amenities abound. There are two swimming pools—one with a bar in it—and a wading pool overlooking the beach, a large hot tub, a fully equipped fitness center, and six tennis courts. Guests may play golf at the 18-hole course at nearby *Kiahuna Plantation*. Inside, the public areas mix travertine marble, brass and teak to achieve a sleek, sophisticated look. All the guest rooms have a sitting area set off from the bed by a bamboo panel, a wet bar, and a brass basin in the marble-topped bathroom vanity, as well as big, thick towels. The hotel's social staff offers lessons in Hawaiian crafts, conducts garden tours, and serves afternoon tea in the spacious library.

The Waiohai Tamarind Restaurant, *above, is the best on the island. Oriental lamps, etched glass, and Thai silk banners set the stage for elegant dining. The cuisine is nouvelle with an Oriental touch; the smoked duck and firecracker shrimp are specialities. Fresh island fish is outstanding. Gourmets also flock to Sunday brunch on the ocean-side terrace where omelets are made to order and island specialties abound. Swimming pools glisten, right, amid the hotel's lush gardens.*

There's something almost sinful about sitting by a pool with
your back turned to one of the best beaches in the islands,
above. But de gustibus non est disputandum, as it were.
For one wishing to sample the pure pleasures of snorkeling
or scuba diving, there is no better beach and no better staff
from which to learn. The water is calm and clear, and the
rocks and reefs abound with fish. One of the most difficult
tasks here is to take a photograph of someone who is not
relaxing. A guest, left, catches up on his reading by the
pool, his business problems a light year or two away.

KIAHUNA PLANTATION

Another perfectly delightful way to enjoy the *Poipu Beach* area is to rent one of the handsome condominiums at *Kiahuna Plantation*, white plantation-style buildings set on 50 of the most beautiful acres anywhere. There are sweeping, manicured lawns, trees and bougainvillea, and lush gardens. Pathways with Japanese-style bridges lead to the beach. The apartments have tall louvered windows and high ceilings making air conditioning unnecessary. Depending on the location, the sound of the surf or the smell of the flowers will sweeten your dreams. The apartments are extra large with redwood-trimmed white walls and decorated with pastel prints and rattan furniture. The kitchens are fully equipped, including dishwashers. If one chooses to eat out, the resort's restaurant, *Plantation Gardens*, is among the finest on Kauai. Housed in an appealing 19th-century plantation manor, it specializes in sea food: sashimi, oysters, crab, shrimp and lobster, plus, of course, the fresh catch of the day. Light lunches and snacks are to be found at the courtside cafe at the 10-court tennis complex. The *Kiahuna* has daily maid service, a pool, and, as a bonus, guests pay no green fees on the two excellent golf courses.

A water lily graces a pool in one of the plantation's lovely gardens, top. Near the beach sunbathers bask, above right, in front of one of the attractive three-unit condominiums. A bit of Polynesian history forms an unusual trap on the championship course. Traces of an ancient village are to be found throughout the plantation area.

KOKEE STATE PARK AND LODGE

Eight miles after the last Waimea Canyon lookout is Kokee State Park: 4,600 acres of some of the most beautiful unspoiled wilderness anywhere. There are more than a dozen hiking trails in the park, totaling 45 miles. They lead through forests of koa, redwood, and pine, and a profusion of mokihana, hibiscus, and maile. (Kauai brides make their wedding *leis* from the vine and berries of maile.) In July and August, you can sample the small, tart plums that grow wild here, and take home up to ten pounds of them with the permission of the park rangers. Forest birds abound and chances are you'll see wild goats. Most trails lead to great views and ideal picnic spots. At the end of the park is the Kalalau Valley Lookout at 4,000 feet elevation. Drive or hike there for a view of the valley opening out to the sea. *Kokee Lodge* has eight cabins of varying sizes, all equipped with kitchens, showers, and fireplaces,that sleep up to eight people. They may be rented for a maximum of four nights at *$25 per cabin*. At these rates they are extremely popular and must be reserved months in advance. There's a little restaurant and general store at the lodge and a small natural history museum next door that's worth a visit.

Awaiting you along the hiking trails
are such delights as this waterfall, left.
Chickens like these, above, roam near
the lodge cabins. Brought from Tahiti
in ancient times, they were
everywhere in the islands at one time
When the mongoose was introduced to
Hawaii to control the rats (a failure:
the mongoose is a day creature, asleep
when the rats are active) it feasted on
the eggs of Tahitian chickens and
other ground-nesting birds, driving
them into extinction. Through
foresight or dumb luck, Kauai was the
only island that did not participate in
the Great Mongoose Experiment.

WAIMEA CANYON

Rumor has it that Samuel Clemens first called *Waimea Canyon* "the Grand Canyon of the Pacific" though there is no record of his ever visiting Kauai. There is a resemblance, however. *Waimea Canyon* is smaller, only 14 1/2 miles long and about 2,800 feet deep, though quite large for a small, subtropical island. Like the Grand Canyon, its steep, multi-layered walls are shaped by erosion and are beautifully colored in varying shades of red and blue. Both have rivers, although the Waimea River is tame compared to the Colorado. There are differences. Waimea gets much more rainfall than the Grand Canyon, and it is covered by vegetation except where its walls are too steep to support it. *Waimea* lies beneath the high mountain-top swamp of the *Alakai*, and sparkling water pours down into the canyon in thin streams with free falls of as much as 200 feet. There are two entries: the *Waimea Canyon Road* starts at *Waimea* and winds through sugar cane fields. The *Kokee Road* begins at *Kekaha* and goes through dry, scrubby land. The lookouts afford stunning views; don't miss one, even if they are crowded. A few miles before the first lookout is the *Kukui Trail* which leads to the bottom of the canyon. It is five miles down and back and there is an overnight shelter at the bottom.

Rainbows are a common sight in Waimea Canyon, top, as rain alternates with luminous sunshine. At Waimea, where the Waimea River meets the sea, island royalty made their summer headquarters. Here Captain Cook in 1778 first landed in Hawaii. Opposite, the "Grand Canyon of the Pacific" enchants visitors with its rugged cliffs and subtle shadings of colors.

PACIFIC TROPICAL BOTANICAL GARDEN

Every three days another species of plant becomes extinct. Botanists believe if the present trend continues, 40,000—one-sixth of the 240,000 plants greening our planet—could be lost forever in the next 40 years. To slow down this alarming attrition is the *raison d'être* of the *Pacific Tropical Botanical Garden*, chartered by Congress in 1964 to collect, study, and cultivate tropical plants with an emphasis on rare and endangered species. More than two-thirds of the known plant species are in the tropics. Lending an even greater urgency to the garden's work are facts like these: several recently discovered tropical plants show promise in the treatment of cancer; a wild relative of corn found in 1977 is perennial and resistent to most domestic corn diseases. The garden's collection includes 500 species of palms, 50 varieties of bananas, and 100 of the 115 species of the coral tree (Erythrina). There is a rare double coconut from the Seychelles that produces 50-pound coconuts, the largest seeds in the world. Botanists here feel they have begun to realize the potential of the garden, an effort that is supported entirely by grants and private donations.

Guiding visitors through the botanical and Allerton gardens is the pleasant task of Marc Code, above. Parts of the garden have the look and feel of a subtropical jungle. Below, bougainvillea gives a splash of riotous color to a dense glade. Tababoulia, better known as the gold tree, is a dazzler in the midday sun, opposite. Botanists come from around the world to study varieties of endangered tropical plants being grown under controlled conditions, and to report on special problems encountered in their own countries.

Moreton Bay Fig (Ficus macrophylla)

An endangered species: Brighamia citrina (Napaliense)

White lotus of Egypt (Nymphaea lotus)

Amaryllis (Hippeastrum hybrid)

Canna lily (Canna generalis)

Licuala grandis

Yellow water poppy (Hydrocleys numphoide)

ALLERTON GARDENS

By the sea and adjoining the *Pacific Tropical Botanical Gardens* is the estate and gardens of Robert Allerton, a wealthy Chicago banker, and his son, John Greg Allerton, an architect. These gardens are a combination of formal gardens and tropical jungle, and have no purpose except beauty. (They are only open to the public as part of the botanical garden tour.) Interesting uses of natural settings abound. In the *Thanksgiving Room*, for instance, the walls are formed by panax trees, whose slim trunks were used by Tahitians to support vanilla bean vines. Flanking a classical water fountain, two monkeypod trees form a sheltering roof. The elder Mr. Allerton provided the initial $1.5 million dollars to start the botanical gardens, and has made additional endowments since. His will leaves the estate and gardens to the botanical garden with the stipulation that they be kept in their present exquisite state and not converted for experimental uses. Mr. Allerton, a gentlemen in his eighties, rode out Hurricane Iwa at his estate, moving to higher ground when his mansion was inundated with four feet of water.

A guide shows a visitor through the tropical jungle part of the Allerton Gardens, opposite. This little cottage, top, is next to the mansion but predates it. It was built by Queen Emma, wife of King Kamehameha IV, who started the gardens a century ago. Statues representing the Four Seasons, above, were blown over by Hurricane Iwa but now stand serenely again.

AROUND KAUAI

There has always been a remote quality about Kauai, the westernmost of the major Hawaiian Islands. It was the last of the islands to be united under the rule of King Kamehameha. It was slow to develop facilities for visitors, and is still mostly rural. But Kauai is perhaps the most beautiful and varied and the most Hawaiian of all the islands. Perhaps that is why so many movies have been filmed here, in whole or in part: the remakes of *Mutiny on the Bounty* and *King Kong*, the jungle sequences of *Raiders of the Lost Ark*, parts of *South Pacific*, and Elvis Presley's *Blue Hawaii*. Sharp-eyed visitors will recognize scenes used in the opening sequences of each episode of *Fantasy Island*. Tom Sellek and his cohorts of *Magnum P.I.* are often filmed here. But, strangely, there is no sense of show business on Kauai. Rather the island is tranquil, visitors relaxing while quiet, happy residents go about their business. The mood changed abruptly, though, two days before Thanksgiving 1982 when *Hurricane Iwa* (named for a mythological Hawaiian bird) struck from the southwest. For more than two hours winds that exceeded 170 miles per hour and 35-foot waves battered the island. Miraculously, no one was killed but property damage exceeded $100 million. Kauai is back in shape now, and a first-time visitor might just miss seeing evidence of the worst storm to hit in a generation.

Every native Kauaian has a hurricane story to tell, or a commemorative T-shirt, opposite top left. An underground lava tube creates this geyser, a blow hole on the South Coast, opposite top middle. A research facility cleverly disguised as the world's largest golf ball, opposite top right. Frequent service to Kauai is provided by Aloha Airlines. In Hanalei, the Bounty House, shaped like a sailing ship, was built by Lewis Milestone, director of Mutiny on the Bounty, below right. Kauai has some of the best snorkeling in the world. A Catholic church, below left, cautions its parishioners in English and Hawaiian.

SOME CHOICE RESTAURANTS

The *Koloa Broiler* lets *you* be the cook. Broil your own steak, chicken, fish, or hamburger, then stop by the salad bar. The *Koloa Ice House* is great for a light lunch or dinner and the only place on he island for bagels and lox. In Lihue, the penthouse restaurant at the *Kauai Surf,* the *Golden Horn* serves up Continental favorites and Oriental dishes with equal panache. The *Hanamaula Restaurant and Tea House* serves a mixture of Cantonese and Szechwan, plus some Japanese dishes for good measure. The local Chinese eat here and it's a bargain. In Wailua, *Don's Deli and Picnic Basket* in the Coconut Plantation Market Place is the place to stock up for a picnic on the beach. And for the best macadamia nut cookies anywhere, head for the *Acme Bakery* in Koloa.

PRINCEVILLE

Princeville is a golfer's paradise, its 27-hole *Makai* course, right, both beautiful and challenging. The course and several attractive condominium complexes share an 11,000-acre estate on Hanalei Bay. Two top places to stay are the *Makai Club Cottages*, below, and *Pali Ke Kua*, both offering hotel services: front desk, daily maid, and charging privileges at the resort's restaurants and shops. The *Makai Club Cottages* are the more spacious. Both the one- and two-bedroom apartments have huge living rooms with fireplaces, separate dining rooms, fully equipped kitchens and dressing rooms and Japanese futo baths. *Pali Ke Kua*, offering the same amenities, is on a cliff a path down to the beach. From most anywhere in Princeville, beautiful mist-shrouded Mount Waialeale can be seen. Princeville is remote and one usually eats in the area. Good choices include: *Bali Hai* for seafood, *Chuck's Steakhouse* for beef, and *Tahiti Nui* to share *luau* fare with the local residents on Friday nights throughout the year.

The first stern New England missionaries arrived in the Hawaiian Islands in 1820. By the middle 1800s, most of the natives had been Christianized and at least partially Westernized, and mainland church groups were beginning to cut off financial support. Sons of the missionaries began looking for material rather than spiritual rewards. Happily for them, the King now was selling off large parcels of land for small amounts, even giving land to those who caught his fancy. "The missionaries taught us how to raise our eyes to Heaven," quips entertainer Do Ho, "and when we looked down the land was gone." For many missionary sons, the pot at the end of their rainbow was filled with sugar. The first fortunes were made in sugar during the California Gold Rush of 1849. As the years passed, great fortunes also were made in pineapples and ranching, but great fortunes bring great problems. The plantation and ranch owners had two: one, they needed a large steady supply of men who would do stoop labor for low wages, for the Hawaiians, although good workers, were self-supporting; and two, they didn't trust the government, fearing the loss of their land in some political upheaval. They solved the first problem by pressuring the government to make laws permitting the importation of laborers. The first group of Chinese came in 1852, followed by waves of Japanese, Portuguese, Filipinos, and Koreans. The second was solved by the 1887 overthrow of the government, setting the stage for the 1898 United States annexation of Hawaii.

KAUAI BY HELICOPTER

To truly experience the grandeur of Kauai, one must view the island from a helicopter. Not only are there places that can be seen no other way—the rain forest of Mount Waialeale and parts of the Na Pali coast—but by condensing the time frame the stunning contrasts on the island are accentuated. In a way, it is like watching a stop-frame motion picture of a flower blooming. Black lava cliffs and tan beaches give way to the green of tropic vegetation then to the pastels of Waimea Canyon. Several helicopter services offer tours but there is none to match Papillon Helicopters. Based at the airport two miles from Princeville, Papillon has four different tours, ranging in price and time from *The Discover* which includes an overview of Waimea Canyon and the Na Pali coast to *The Odyssey* which covers all of Kauai and a flight back in time to the nearby Forbidden Island of Nihau, including a picnic stop. Passengers wear earphones to hear special music and the pilot's informed commentary.

A helicopter flies low through Waimea Canyon, above. Wainiha Bay, near Haena, inset. The massive Waimea Canyon was sculpted by the thin, silvery Waimea River, rising in the Alakai Swamp, and fed by Mt. Waialeale.

The upper slope of Mount Waialeale is the wettest place on earth, with an average rainfall of 450 inches. Dozens of waterfalls carry this deluge to the valley below.

The rugged, uninhabited Na Pali coast can be reached only by helicopter and Zodiac boat. Traces of 1,200-year-old Polynesian settlements have been found here.

MAUI

"It was the sublimest spectacle I ever witnessed and the memory of it will remain with me always."

Samuel Langhorne Clemens
writing on the Haleakala Crater

HYATT REGENCY MAUI

The newest hotel on Kaanapali Beach is this $80-million, 815-room extravaganza from· developer Chris Hemmeter who created the *Hyatt Regency Waikiki*. Mr. Hemmeter again on an even grander scale, and again fun is the keynote. There's a 100-year-old banyan tree growing in the middle of the atrium lobby. Greenery cascades from on high in two corners. Oriental art is everywhere, a collection valued at $2 million. Outside, a mile-long network of streams and waterfalls (60 varying sizes) interlaces a Japanese garden. Exotic birds are everywhere; there is a full-time ornithologist on the staff. The pool is huge, gorgeous, and lounges near it are *the* place to be seen. There are five restaurants: the *Swan Court* is elegance personified, the *Lahaina Provision Company* is more casual, *Spats II* swings with the same disco abandon as its Waikiki counterpart. There is a waterslide two-and-a-half stories high, a bar that is reached by swimming under a waterfall, a 55-foot catamaran, a health club, tennis courts, volleyball in the swimming pool, a flashy Polynesian show. In fact, it has everything.

Some people go to a resort to get away from it all, some to get to it all. The latter category will find the Hyatt Regency Maui *a giant candy store. The proprietor is general manager Bill Rhodes, shown, opposite top, in the atrium lobby. He's rarely seen with a parrot on his shoulder but he does have much to smile about. Even Kaanapali Beach has a hard time competing for attention with the resort's pool, opposite bottom, and the landscaping complements both. Even Hollywood in its glory days couldn't come up with a finer setting than the Swan Court, above left. Imagine a Fred Astaire-Ginger Rogers number starting at their lagoon-side table as a pair of rather unusual swans, above right, glide by. The Kiele V, a custom built catamaran, has a snorkeling cruise in the morning with a continental breakfast, refreshments, and a deli lunch; a cocktail sail in the late afternoon. In the winter months there's a chance of spotting a humpback whale. But if snorkeling and whales and sunsets aren't your cup of tea, you can always get comfortable and watch the two-girl crew, one of whom is pictured at left, going about their tasks.*

LAHAINA

Whaling made this waterfront town, once the summer residence of Maui high chiefs. By 1846, 429 whalers were putting into port here in their pursuit of the whales that winter in these waters. Missionaries in town grew apoplectic at the sight of hundreds of sailors seeking grog and women after months at sea. When the good townspeople closed grog shops and forbade native women to visit the ships, riots broke out. One whaler fired a few cannonballs into a reverend's yard. Nothing was settled when the discovery of oil in Pennsylvania and the Civil War ended the whaling era. Lahaina declined and did not recover until the tourist boom. The whalers left Lahaina a colorful legacy; its new life as a let-it-all-hang-out sort of place gives the town colors of a different hue.

In one of the town's historic buildings, Andrew Walker's Lahaina Printsellers Ltd., top, offers old maps and prints, including some made from drawings by Captain Cook's shipboard artist. On the outskirts of town, above, a minister's prophecy strikes an incongruous note.

The restored vessel Carthaginian II, *opposite, is the only reminder of what the harbor must have been like once. Sailors often spent the night in the old jail, above. A story has it that a sailor brought a box of mosquitos here in retribution for his incarceration.*

114

PIONEER INN

"*Women is not allowed in you room. If you wet or burn bed you going out. You are not allowed to gambel in you room. You are not allow in the down stears … when you are drunk. You must use a shirt when you come to seating room.*" These stern house rules dating from the inn's opening in 1901 suggest a somewhat rowdy clientele. The *Pioneer Inn* is one of Lahaina's most famous landmarks and still is very much in business today. The original structure faces the harbor, behind it is a new wing added in 1966 which looks just as authentic. (The air-conditioned new wing, most important here, is the nicer place to stay.) There's a swimming pool, beautiful bay views, and three restaurants. The *Harpooner's Lanai* is the best spot in town for breakfast.

A life-size carving of a whaler stands on the porch of the inn, left. From the second-story verandah, below, one can still see a whale spouting from time to time. A favorite watering-hole in Lahaina is the Pioneer Inn Saloon, *bottom. It's jammed at night with those who have come to hear the jazz piano of David Paquette. The walls of the saloon (and much of the hotel) are full of memorabilia of the days when whalers filled the town's bay.*

The Blue Max *opposite top, does nice things with fresh fish and its steak Diane is renowned. Other good dining places in Lahaina include* Kimo's *for the largest piece of prime ribs imaginable, and a fine ocean view;* Longhi's *for pasta and dessert (they claim to have created a thousand different desserts);* Hamburger Mary's Organic Grill *for the burgers and super salads;* Banyan Inn *for the Portuguese bean soup and bargain prices; and* Su Casa *for the best Mexican food in West Maui.*

Every winter humpback whales come from the Gulf of Alaska to mate and give birth to their young. From 500 to 800 of these leviathans make for the shallow area bounded by Maui, Lanai, and Molokai. Humpbacks range from 40 to 50 feet in length and weigh about 30 tons.

AN ANCIENT ART LIVES ON

The origins of the art and practice of tattooing are lost in the mists of time. The Polynesian men and women who greeted Captain Cook were tattooed, so the roots go deep. The very word tattoo is from the Tahitian term *tatau.* The Maoris of New Zealand who came here in their long canoes were tattooed. (The young man, top left, giving the Maori tongue-wagging greeting has painted the traditional markings on his face.) Some tattoos had meanings; the markings of a warrior, say or of mourning. (Queen Liholiho had a ritual line tattooed on her tongue as a sign of mourning.) Ritual tattoos are now found only in the most primitive part of the world but tattoos as decoration have continued to thrive. Many servicemen passing through Hawaii to Pacific wars had themselves tattooed as a rite of passage. There is no finer tattooist in the islands today than Taunee Beeckman, above left, who has an attractive parlor in Lahaina, *Skin Deep.* Born in Minnesota she learned her craft as an apprentice in Houston then went to Alaska to tattoo pipeline workers before setting up shop here. She does both original traditional designs, and the thin lines and delicate colorings of her work show a strong Japanese influence, opposite. One of her specialties is incorporating an old, fading tattoo, often crudely done, into a brilliant new design. (She also has developed a technique of tattooing tiny flowers and other designs on women's fingernails. It's painless and impermanent: the tattoo slowly vanishes as the nail grows.) Are tattoos becoming a thing of the past? A straw in the wind, perhaps, was noted at the annual fair at Honolulu's *Punahou School.* One of the most popular booths had children standing in line to have fanciful designs applied to their faces, top right, that would remain, probably, until their evening bath.

THE SUGAR CANE TRAIN

The Lahaina Kaanapali & Pacific Rail-Road, the *Sugar Cane Train*, takes passengers on a 12-mile round-trip through Hawaiian history. During the run from Kaanapali and back the conductor tells of the importance of sugar cane to the islands and how it was transported by train to the mill, sometimes accompanying himself on a ukulele. It's all a reconstruction, but loads of fun.

Engineer Sergio Cabanting, above, is all business when taking the train over the 415-foot Hahakea Trestle, above right, and the passengers show the photographer they're having a grand time. The trip can be combined with a Lahaina tour, lunch, and even a glass-bottom boat ride.

KAPALUA BAY HOTEL & VILLAS

Kapalua is the best golf resort in the islands but if it had no golf course it still would be a world-class resort. To understand *Kapalua*, a bit of history is in order. In the mid 1970's, Colin C. Cameron hired a team of resort experts to turn 750 of his family-owned 23,000 acres into as fine a resort as they could create. They did him proud. The hotel, golf courses and condominiums were designed to take advantage of the setting and complement one another. (In 1978, a party was held for selected prospects for the unbuilt condominiums. When it was over, 32 out of 40 had been sold at some $14 million. The rest were gone in a week.) The 198-room, $30-million hotel is small by Hawaiian standards (the *Hilton Hawaiian Village* has 2,612 rooms), the comfortable, spacious rooms have private *lanais*, the complex includes five bays and three sandy beaches, a ten-court Tennis Garden, several chic places to dine, etc. But back to golf. First, your golf bag is taken to the club house when you check in, and you *literally* don't have to touch it again till you check out. (Your clubs and shoes will be cleaned without asking.) Second, guests are not charged green fees or cart rentals. You may play until you drop every day of your holiday. Third, although resort golf club houses can be intimidating, everyone in the *Kapalua* golf operation treats you like an old friend. Last, but hardly least, are the two 18-hole courses. The *Bay Course*, an Arnold Palmer-Francis Duane design, climbs a mountain then swings back toward the ocean, passing through a field of pineapples. It is a forgiving, beautiful course. The tough *Village Course* (Arnold Palmer again with Ed Seay) will bring out the best or the worst in any golfer. Both are breathtaking with Lanai and Molokai looming magestically across the blue water.

A waiter navigates the bridge, opposite top, over the pool that sparkles in the hotel's atrium. At the pool, opposite center, an early riser ponders whether or not to take the plunge. Famed Hawaiian artist Pegge Hopper's murals (part of one is shown, opposite below) are a perfect decorative touch in the Plantation Veranda, a speciality restaurant that features such delectables as a selection of home-made pâté, a bouillabaisse made with local fresh fish, and as good a selection of California wines as can be found west of California. The beach, top, is a few palm trees down from the hotel. (If the hotel's architecture seems familiar, you've seen the Kahala Hilton on Oahu; Edward Killingsworth designed both.) With the aerobic instructor, left, as a role model, one could face the morning workout with pleasure. Craig Williamson, director of golf, runs a model operation. In early November the top pros come here for the Kapalua International. The prize money is big and it's televised.

El Crab Catcher, *above, is an excellent restaurant (try the crab-stuffed mushrooms), draws an attractive clientele, and is* the *place on Kaanapali Beach for girl-watching. A beauty of quite a different sort is the Iao Needle, opposite, which stretches 2,250 feet above the Iao Valley State Park. In this serene valley in 1790 Kamehameha fought the battle that won him Maui, one of the bloodiest battles in the history of the islands. When it was over the Iao Stream, also opposite, was filled with dead warriors and the water ran red. The park is near Wailuku, offering easy hiking trails and great places to picnic.*

STOUFFER'S WAILEA BEACH HOTEL

There are two major resort areas on Maui: Kaanapali and Wailea and both have their loyal following. Wailea is smaller, quieter, and has a more sophisticated elegance. The premier resort here is *Stouffer's Wailea Beach Hotel*, until recently owned by Westin. This world-class resort is artfully designed for those who want to be far from the madding crowd *but* with all the creature comforts close at hand. It has only 350 rooms but feels even more intimate. The airy public areas are spacious and the landscaping is masterful, with gardens, waterfalls, and winding paths leading to nice visual surprises. The well-appointed rooms are large and the beach cottages are exceptional. *Raffles*, the hotel's specialty restaurant, is the finest in the area. The *Maui Onion* is a poolside delight with white thunbergia vines hanging overhead. Two of the best golf courses in Hawaii are available to guests, the Blue and the Orange Courses. The Orange is the more challenging, its 6,810 yards a Jack Snyder design. Red-blossomed *wiliwili* trees dot the course and buttonwood trees are the 150-yard markers. There are 5 beaches in the resort area, a shopping center, and an 11-court tennis complex.

INTER-CONTINENTAL MAUI

Wailea Beach is a totally planned resort area and it is a masterpiece. In 1970, it was conceived by the landowners Alexander and Baldwin, two of Hawaii's Big Five. First came a golf course, then two hotels, a second golf course, three condominium villages, a tennis complex and a shopping center. And in the process 1,450 acres of scrubland has been transformed into 1,450 acres of rolling greenery. The *Inter-Continental Maui*, built in 1976, was the first hotel to go up and the sheer quality of its architecture and landscaping, below, helped set the tone for everything that followed. It is a five-minute walk along the beach from *Stouffer's Wailea Beach Hotel*, and with 600 rooms is nearly twice as large as its neighbor. Half of the rooms are in six charming low-rise buildings around the grounds, the remainder in the seven-story tower. There is an air of relaxed luxury everywhere. The long, elegant lobby is open to the air with fountains, potted greens and cosy seating areas. There are three swimming pools, and guests share the golf courses and tennis courts. There is an extensive water sports program. One of *Maui's* finest restaurants is the hotel's *La Perouse*, named after an early French explorer of the islands. The room is paneled in *koa* wood, the chairs upholstered in suede, and a harpist plays at dinner. The speciality here is seafood but the lamb, beef and veal entrees are not to be overlooked. A perfect way to begin is with the breadfruit vichyssoise.

DA O.K. KINE CORALL

PARK YOUR HORSE AND BROWSE

Home, home on the range in Upland Maui, top, horses graze in a distinctly non-Hawaiian setting. A cactus, above left, looks out to sea. When the Wild West collides with Hawaiian pidgin', above right, syntax and spelling suffer but the meaning is clear. At the headquarters of the 30,000-acre Ulupalakua Ranch, right, a model of a cowpoke stands guard.

UPCOUNTRY MAUI

The lower slopes of Haleakala are known as the Upcountry. Sugar cane and pineapple fields give way to clumps of cactus and grazing lands for horses and cattle. A few Hawaiian touches remain: fields of cultivated flowers and vast panoramas of the Pacific, but there's more a sense of the Wild West than West Maui. It's cooler up here, in the low 70's during the day, often chilly at night. The Upcountry is great farm country, too, and produces two crops for which the island is justly famous: *Maui onions*, sweet and toothsome as a ripe apple, and the Irish potatoes from which are made *Maui potato chips*, quite simply the best chips anywhere. The Tedeschi Vineyards are beginning to market their first still and sparkling wines locally. A first tasting of a Tedeschi sparkling white showed fine promise, hardly a *Dom Pérignon* but with a potential to equal the better California wines, full bodied and slightly fruity.

An octagonal church, top, was built in 1897 in Pukalani to serve Portuguese ranch and farm hands. At the Tedeschi Winery, above, a pineapple wine, right, was produced while serious attempts at viniculture went on. The winery once was the jail for the Ulupalakua Ranch.

131

HEAVENLY HANA

A stone lion guards the gates to *Heavenly Hana*, a small, Japanese-style inn on the Hana Highway between the airport and town. The grounds show the imagination and craftsmanship of a Japanese gardner. The lobby is filled with Japanese *objets d'art*. Behind *soji* screens are four rental units, comfortable and more Western in style. They contain two double bedrooms, a small sitting room with television, a kitchen with refrigerator and hot plate, a bathroom with stall shower, and a porch. No swimming pool. No meals are served but there is talk that this might change. *Heavenly Hana* is a charming and inexpensive alternative in the area and perfectly convenient if one has a car. Call ahead for reservations, the management has been known to be erratic.

In a grotto along the Hana Highway, a lei-draped madonna kneels serenely, right. White-faced Herefords graze on a hill near Hana, below. The road twists and turns so sharply that suddenly coming on a waterfall, right, is a special treat. Look closely, above center, and you can see it amidst the scenery and the turn it has just negotiated. T-shirts proclaim: "I survived the road to Hana."

TO HANA AND BEYOND

After manuevering the tortuous road to Hana, the town itself is a letdown. The road smooths, you see a church or two, a school, a shopping center, a few houses and, suddenly, you're at the other end of town. But the attraction is the Hana area, not Hana itself. George Harrison, Jim Nabors, Kris Kristofferson, Burt Reynolds, Carol Burnett and other show-business luminaries live in the neighborhood so there must be some reason Hana is so special. (There is no see-the-homes-of-the-stars tour here; your chance of seeing someone famous is slight.) Perhaps Hana'a magic lies in its very Hawaiianness. This was an area of strategic importance in the years before Kamehameha the Great united the islands. Attacks on neighboring islands were launched from Hana; invaders from other islands landed here. There were big battles waged. "The Hawaiian vibes are very strong," said one young resident. Rest from the trip and then explore. The *Hasegawa General Store* (the title and subject of a zany island song), right below, has an inventory that packs the store from floor to ceiling and can fill all your needs. Actually your tour starts here: across the street is a famous battleground, and reports tell the story of a thousand war canoes arriving from the Big Island. A favorite stop is the *Seven "Sacred" Pools*, top right, more properly known as the *Seven Pools of Kipahulu*. The swimming is great but the rocks are slippery. By legend, "the sky comes close to Hana," and on the cinder cone called *Kauki Hill*, right center, a Hawaiian god once stood and flung his spear through the sky. Hana is a reminder of what all Hawaii once was like.

133

HOTEL HANA MAUI

Guests seem to return here with the regularity of the swallows to Capistrano. Between visits they receive a newsletter, *Mano O Hana* (The Spirit of Hana), filled with such items as a busboy's marriage, or the repaving of the driveway. There is a framed chart with photographs in the lobby showing, apparently, that most of the employees are related and have been at the hotel all their working lives. Built in 1946 as a ranch, the hotel now has a scattering of one-story buildings around the grounds that contain 60 guest rooms, and a two-story guest cottage near the main building. This is the only serious hotel in Hana, and the dining room the only serious restaurant. (If you see one of the celebrities who live in Hana, chances are it will be in the dining room or bar here.) There is a heated swimming pool on the grounds and private facilities at beautiful *Hamoa Beach*, right center, three miles away. The stable is excellent and the hotel is deservedly popular with riders. If you fly to Hana, you'll be picked up at the airport by the hotel's 1929 Packard station wagon, right top, and chances are lovely Michelle Wilhelm, opposite, will be waiting to greet you in the handsome lobby, below. On checking in you will be given a copy of *Pupu Call*, "your good fun guide while at Heavenly Hana," which lists an awesome array of activities, which most guests ignore.

THE LONE EAGLE: R.I.P.

Charles Lindbergh piloted *The Spirit of St. Louis* from Mineola, New York, to Paris in May 1927 to become the first person to fly the Atlantic non-stop and alone. He was nicknamed "the Lone Eagle" and was the greatest hero in an age of heros. Sadly, he was a private man, never comfortable with his fame. He spent the last years of his life on his beloved Maui where he died August 24, 1974. He was buried near his home at the tiny *Kipahulu Hawaiian Church*, below, where a window with a Hawaiian vision of Christ looks out toward the sea. Lindbergh was buried in a traditional Hawaiian grave, a rock-filled square surrounding the simple headstone. The church and grounds are touchingly poignant, but unmarked and hard to find. His friends and neighbors want Lindbergh to have here the peace and quiet that was denied him in his lifetime. A few tiny American flags are the only echoes of the cheers that once greeted him wherever he went.

"Midway across the North Pacific, space, time and life
uniquely interlace a chain of islands named 'Hawaiian' . . .
The small fragments of land appear offered to sky by water
and pressed to earth by stars."

Charles A. Lindbergh

LANAI

''Those long beaches are enticing to the idle man.''
Robert Louis Stevenson

HOTEL LANAI

The *Hotel Lanai* is the *only* hotel on Lanai. Even if there were more, it would be hard to top this one because the hotel's president, Alberta de Jetley (right, getting a peck from her pet parrot) learned the art of making a hotel more than a place to sleep and eat from her late husband who made the *Hana Maui* into a world-class resort. The *Hotel Lanai*, below, was built in 1927 to house the guests and visiting executives of Dole whose pineapple fields cover 19,000 acres. It has 10 guest rooms and a two-bedroom cottage. Ms. de Jetley has renovated the hotel with imaginative good taste and the food in the wood paneled dining room is appetizing. The enclosed lanai is the only bar in Lanai City—the total population of the island is only 2,100—and guests mingle with the local gentry. Lanai remained uninhabited for nearly a thousand years after the Polynesians arrived in the islands. They believed evil spirits lived here. The island was used for cattle grazing and fishing until 1920 when Jim Dole bought it for $1.1 million and created the world's largest pineapple plantation. (A visitor, opposite, spots something interesting on the rocks at Manele Bay.)

Pineapples are synonymous with Hawaii yet none grew here until the early 1800s, and none were grown and sold commercially until James D. Dole planted 60 acres on Oahu in 1899. The fruit was first found in the West Indies and South America by Spanish explorers who called them *piñas*! because they resembled pine cones. Soon pineapples were growing throughout much of the world, but nowhere do they grow as delicious as here. Despite modern equipment, the harvesting is stoop labor and women do the stooping. Wearing gloves, masks, boots and heavy protective clothing, they walk between the rows, picking the ripe fruit, and putting it on a conveyor belt that empties into a huge, slow-moving truck-like vehicle, below. During the harvest, on Lanai, crews like this pick as many as a million pineapples a day. It is hot, hard work but the women are unionized and the pay is good. And a snug company cottage, right, awaits them after a long day in the fields.

DESERTED VILLAGE

There are 25 miles of paved roads on Lanai, most of them running through the pineapple fields, and to really see the island a four-wheel-drive vehicle and adequate time are required. This is not an island for those who wish to breeze in air-conditioned comfort from one interesting spot to another. Hardy lovers of out-of-doors, though, revel in its beauty and the serendipities they encounter. One is found by driving straight on where the paved road ends at *Shipwreck Beach.* In the woods are a deserted church, opposite, and a whaleboat, above, all that remains of *Keomuku Village*, which once had pretensions of rivaling Lahaina, across the *Auau Channel* on Maui. It was starting to thrive as a sugar plantation when, in 1901, the irrigation water turned brackish. The dream of growing cane on Lanai vanished as did the town. All the buildings, except, for some reason, the church, were dismantled and shipped to Lahaina. Perhaps Lahaina had enough churches; it certainly had enough whale boats.

145

In Hawaiian, lanai *means "hump"
and the hump that gave this island its
name is* Lanaihale, *a mountain that
rises sharply at its southern end,
reaching a height of 3,370 feet before
descending to the sea. The* Munro
Trail *runs along its ridge and it's a
tough, rough jeep ride in the best of
conditions. It rewards the adventurous
with vistas, left, that are unforgetable.
On a clear day all the islands, except
Kauai and Nihau, can be seen from
the summit. (The trail is named after
a New Zealander who managed the
ill-fated cattle-raising experiment on
the island. An amateur botanist, he
planted the tall Norfolk pines that now
are seen everywhere here.) An easier
ride is to the* Garden of the Gods,
right, *an area of odd lava formations
and scattered rocks that came from
who knows where. It is both eerie and
beautiful at sunset.*

MOLOKAI

"It was his part, by one striking act of martyrdom, to direct all men's eyes on that distressful colony. At a blow, and with the price of his life, he made the place illustrious . . ."

From an open letter to the
Reverend Dr. Hyde of Honolulu
from Robert Louis Stevenson, 1889

SHERATON MOLOKAI

The roar of the surf on beautiful *Kepuhi Beach* pervades this handsome 29-acre resort in West Molokai, and the rest of the world seems far away. When the *Sheraton Molokai* was built in 1977, it doubled the number of hotel and condominium rooms on the island, which tells you something about Molokai. The rooms here are in one- and two-story buildings along the shore and the golf course. It's more like having your own island home than staying in a hotel. The beach is usually too rough for swimming, but it's a joy to walk. A free-form swimming pool overlooks the ocean. There are two excellent choices for dinner: the *Ohia Lodge* with a view of Oahu 26 miles away, and the *Panilolo Broiler* where steaks are done to a turn over *kiawe* charcoal. (Southwesterner's will recognize the flavor; the *kiawe* tree is first-cousin to the *mesquite*.) The salad bar here is also good, and don't miss the French toast made with Molokai bread. There are four tennis courts, a 15-kilometer jogging trail, horseback riding, and volleyball, but most guests come here for golf. The Ted Robinson championship course is known as *Kalua Koi*. It's quite short (6,177 yards from the men's tees) but will stretch a golfer's ability: lakes and bunkers abound, and the wind can be troublesome. Five holes go along the ocean, and you are apt to run into deer, wild turkey and other game birds, as you progress inland. (Complimentary green fees to hotel guests.) A note of caution: after the Pro Bowl in Honolulu in January, the NFL players association holds its annual meeting and golf tournament here. This has a most disconcerting effect on men of normal stature.

A golfer looks for his ball in the sand, top. By the sea, by the beautiful sea, far left. The main building, left, and the cottages, above, have a Polynesian flavor. It's best to have a rental car here, there's a lot nearby to see.

151

The sea pounds in on Molokai's North shore and a rare monk seal (so-called because of the cowl at the back of its neck) takes temporary refuge on the beach, left. Monk seals share with bats the distinction of being the first mammals in the islands. Nearly slaughtered out of existence, monk seals, protected in Hawaii since 1909, now number about 1,000.

MOLOKAI MULE TRIAN

One of the most unusual and memorable experiences in Hawaii is riding in a mule train on the three-and-one-eighth mile trail that links the *Palaau State Park* on the bluffs with the *Makanalua Peninsula* below. The *Molokai Mule Ride* takes seven hours and includes a box lunch in a lovely setting and a moving tour of the former leper colony at *Kalaupapa*. The ride is well supervised and perfectly safe although the first look down at the peninsula is sure to bring on second thoughts. The ride is not for everyone (minimum age, 16; maximum weight, 225) and there are other ways to visit *Kalaupapa*. Those who do take the ride, though, have the rare combination of an exhilarating physical and moving spiritual experience. Further rewards: a certificate of membership in the *Order of Alii Mule Skinners of Molokai*, and a bumper sticker: "Wouldn't You Rather Be Riding a Mule in Molokai?"

Master guide Buzzy Sproat, above, leads a party on the steep winding Kalaupapa Trail, opposite, an all-day outing. It takes the sure-footed mules longer to go down the trail than come up. Below, neophyte riders are briefed to remember their mule's "Hawaiian" name. Ours: Pale Face.

THE COLONY

In 1936, Ike Kead, right, was a week away from entering the sixth grade in Honolulu when he was diagnosed as a leper. For two bitter years he was a human guinea pig in a program testing possible cures for the disease. His usefulness to the program deemed over, he was sent to the colony here. Leprosy had been renamed Hansen's Disease after the Norwegian physician who isolated the bacillus that caused it in 1874. It wasn't until the 1940s, however, that scientists found that the disease could be arrested by sulfone drugs. Now fewer than a hundred patients remain at the colony, ranging in age from the early 50s to over 80. They are free to go but don't, the life here too ingrained, perhaps, or the problems of re-entering society too formidable. Family and friends sometimes visit. (Many patients married although children born to them were taken away and not allowed back at the colony until they reached 16.) Ike Kead runs *Ike's Scenic Tours* of the colony and the peninsula, alternating between a Don Rickles humor and a candid and poignant view of his life here. The beauty of the beach, below, takes on a new dimension when he describes how the early lepers were dumped here. He uses Father Damien's church as the setting for his moving talk about his life at the colony. A visitor noted a touching detail: in the rest rooms at the colony there are no mirrors.

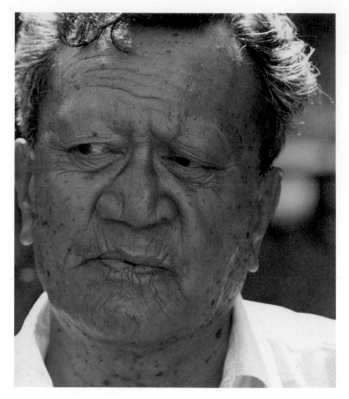

St. Philomena
1889
FATHER DAMIEN
CHURCH

FATHER DAMIEN

In 1863 in Belgium, a novitiate in the Society of the Sacred Heart volunteered to go to Hawaii as a missionary in place of his ailing brother. Joseph de Veuster was 24 when he was ordained a priest in Honolulu, taking the name Father Damien. Leprosy had preceded him to the islands, arriving with the first Chinese laborers sometime in the 1820's, and the disease was called *ma'i Pake*, the Chinese disease. The fear of leprosy was intense. By attacking the nerve ends and muscles of the arms and legs and affecting the skin, it crippled and disfigured its victims. We know now that leprosy was never highly contagious, and rarely fatal. It shortened life by making a victim much more suseptible to tuberculosis and other diseases. But this fear led the Hawaiian government to place the lepers on an isolated peninsula called *Makanalua*, *The Given Grave*, for to be sent here was a death sentence. Boats from ships carried the lepers to shore, those who resisted were thrown overboard. Often a leper made it to shore only to have his few belongings stolen by fellow lepers from the colony. It was a pitiful anarchy. There were no doctors, no help of any kind. This living hell moved Father Damien to volunteer to take spiritual charge of the colony. He arrived at *Makanalua* in 1873, at a time when one or two of the thousand or so lepers living here were dying every day. Besides religion, Father Damien brought energy, organization, and justice. Through his own labors and repeated appeals to the government in Hawaii he was able to get medical assistance, water piped in and better food and shelter for his flock. He made regular trips on foot up and down the cliff and founded several other churches. One Sunday in 1844, at St. Philomea's, his church at the colony, he began his sermon not with the words "My Brethren," but by saying "Fellow lepers." He died five years later, aged 49. He received world-wide attention, particularly through a published letter of Robert Louis Stevenson describing Father Damien as "the father of all of us who love goodness."

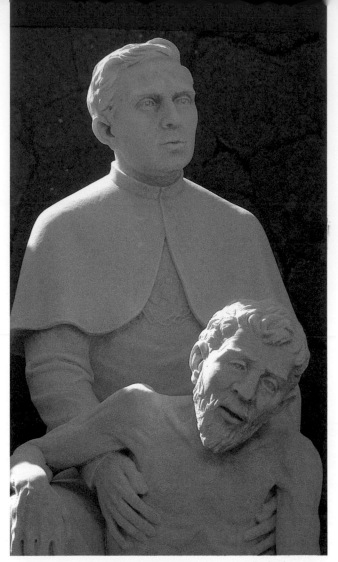

Statues of Father Damien are to be found throughout the islands. The lei-draped one, opposite, stands at the entrance to the state capitol, a duplicate in Statuary Hall in the U.S. Capitol in Washington. The statue, by Marisol, caused a controversy when unveiled in 1969 because it showed him disfigured by leprosy. The Roman Catholic Church has begun the process of canonization of Father Damien.

MOLOKAI RANCH WILDLIFE PARK

More than 300 animals native to India and Africa roam an 800-acre wildlife preserve on the *Molokai Ranch*, a few minutes away from the *Sheraton Molokai*. The preserve was started in 1977 by the ranch to stock and breed rare animals for zoos and parks around the world. There are giraffes, barbary sheep, Indian black buck, sable antlelope, wild turkeys and an ostrich that does a spirited dance for visitors when they arrive at the gate. All thrive in the warm dry climate here and to see a giraffe grazing on a hilltop tree is to believe, at least for a moment, that one has suddenly been transported to Africa. The van tour takes a delightful 90 minutes and there are plenty of opportunities to see the animals up close.

AROUND MOLOKAI

The only way to really see Molokai is in a four-wheel-drive vehicle and there's no better driver-guide-companion than Carl Adopho, top, of *Molokai Adventures.* (If you *really* want to experience the island arrange a camping trip with him.) Among the sights are ancient Polynesian petroglyphs, above. These prehistoric carvings tell the history of a people, of kings and gods, and of voyages in long canoes. At Kaunakakai once stood the summer home of Kamehameha V. During his nine-year-reign (1863–1872) he planted a ten-acre grove of palm trees. Some are gone, but the sight still is impressive, opposite. (A word of caution: in a grove of *coconut* palms don't walk too near the trees. A coconut bouncing off your head can end your vacation abruptly.)

HAWAII

"The ancient Hawaiians drew comfort from a legend that the same great lava flows that occasionally devastated their fields also built up their islands. About a century ago scientific fact began to catch up with the myth."

Robert Wallace

MAUNA KEA BEACH HOTEL

To come right out with it, the *Mauna Kea Beach Hotel* is the finest resort in the islands, if not the world. It has everything a great resort should have, plus some distinctive touches of its own. For example, a near-priceless collection of art from Polynesia and the Far East, more than 1,000 objects, all on display and all adding to the resort's visual impact. Two personal favorites: a dazzling collection of framed Hawaiian quilts, and a 1,500-pound Indian Buddha carved in the seventh century from pink granite. Another example is the Robert Trent Jones, Sr., golf course. One of the most beautiful courses in the islands, it is *the* toughest. It punishes inaccuracy at every opportunity on its long 7,000 yards. And still another is the food. The Sunday brunch is unsurpassed; people come from all over the island to sample its treasures. The standards are equally high and the cuisine as imaginative in the *Dining Pavillion*, *Garden Pavillion*, and *Batik Room*. The superlatives continue: the landscaping is dreamlike, the pool a blue gem, the beach is everything one could want in a beach, and the weather is as fine as the islands can offer. Lawrence S. Rockefeller built *Mauna Kea* in 1965 and lavished his money, his attention, and his love for the environment on it. And it is every bit as great now as the day it opened. As one lovely young guest said, "If this is what Heaven is like, I'm going to be very good."

The beach at Mauna Kea, *above*, is as nice as any on the Big Island. Winter brings waves that provide surfing; the summer waves are little more than a foot high. When the ocean is calm, there is an evening extravaganza: a search-light at the point is trained on the water, luring plankton which in turn attracts giant manta. The graceful, delta-shaped fish then do a water-air ballet that delights guests. CBS Correspondent Jim Jensen, *right*, relaxes after covering the Mauna Loa eruption. *Opposite*, the beauty of a great resort summed up in a single photograph.

168

KONA VILLAGE RESORT

On the site of an ancient Polynesian settlement, *Kona Village* is a colony of individual thatched roof cottages surrounding a crystal-clear bay where once Hawaiians fished and made salt to trade with upland farmers. Every artifice has been used to recapture the feel of Old Hawaii, and discreetly adds modern amenities. The management describes the style as "plush/primitive" and it's as good a description as any. A high-powered San Francisco lawyer put it differently: "This is my alternative to a psychiatrist's couch." The 62-acre enclave is surrounded by thousands of acres of barren lava fields. The cottages look rustic on the outside, invitingly comfortable on the inside: louvered doors, wicker furniture, plants and nice paintings. No telephones, television or newspapers intrude. Relaxation is definitely the key. For the active there are tennis courts, sailboats, miniature golf, volleyball and outrigger canoes. The more sedate can learn about *lei*-making and flower-arranging. The resort is American Plan, the food delicious; fresh fish, beef Wellington, and rack of venison are specialites. Weekly specials include a *paniolo* steak fry, a *luau*, and a seafood buffet.

The cottages, opposite top, come in different styles and all ensure blissful comfort. The view, opposite below, from a lagoon-side cottage. Guests Alex Karras and his actress wife Susan Clark (stars of ABC's Webster) relax in a double hammock. Kona village attracts celebrities: supermodel Christie Brinkley was married here. Contemplation at the beach, left, and a tongue-in-cheek word of caution, below. Social director Kahea Beckley, below left, is a direct descendent of both Kameeiamoku, high chief of the village that once stood here, and Captain George C. Beckley, designer of the state flag. His tour of the petroglyphs here is not to be missed.

MAUNA LANI BAY HOTEL

The newest super-luxury resort on the Kona Coast is the $79-million, 351-room *Mauna Lani Bay Hotel* which opened early in 1983. Arriving here, it is hard not to stop and gawk at the atrium lobby, opposite, as long as a football field, and seemingly skyhigh. (It's a delightful spot for an early-evening drink.) A glass enclosed elevator whisks you to your floor. The high-ceilinged rooms are spacious, with large *lanais*. A ceiling fan is thoughtfully provided for those who prefer natural ventilation. Mahogany shutters grace the rooms. The excellent beach is complemented by manmade lagoons and imaginative landscaping. A scuba boat takes divers to nearby reefs, and a catamaran offers cruises. Also available are small sailboats and windsurfers, Hawaiian canoes, and fishing tackle for shoreline fishing. Jogging trails wind through the grounds. The ten Plexipave-surfaced tennis courts are finished to play at five different speeds to match a player's ability. The *Francis H. I'i Brown Gold Course* is a masterpiece. Named for a world-famous amateur, its 6,813 yards wind through black lava fields on the front nine, brown lava fields on the back nine. If the beauty of the course doesn't distract you, it's comparatively easy, despite 84 sand traps. *Mauna Lani* has four restaurants. The *Bay Terrace* features Puna Papaya Pearls in an orange brandy mist; Chateaubriand Gatti-Gazzaza, two slices of beef, one with Bordelaise, one with Bearnaise sauce; and a superb saddle of lamb. Another choice, *The Third Floor*, is a re-creation of the restaurant at Waikiki's *Regent Hotel*, ranked as one of Hawaii's best.

Abstract sculpture in a fountain, guests in a jacuzzi, top, the good life at the Mauna Lani Bay Hotel *comes in many forms. Once this was a Kona Coast lava field, its blackness stretching from the mountain to the sea, right. Now it is an international playground and a half-dozen languages can be heard around the pool. The heart of the resort is a huge atrium, opposite. Its beauty changes as the sunlight strikes it from different angles during the day. In the early evening, guests gather for cocktails at the foot of the grand staircase, to be serenaded by soft Hawaiian music.*

172

THE KONA COAST

Even when the volcanos are quiet, a drive down the northern part of the Kona Coast is a reminder of their fury. From the Kohola resort areas, where landscaping and irrigation have created lushness, the highway passes through barren black lava fields, a hint, perhaps, of what the world might look like after a nuclear war. To the left are the slopes of *Mauna Kea,* the world's largest single mountain mass. Yet it doesn't *look* like a mountain, rather like a gentle, outsized hill. Its very enormity tricks your senses, the way an elephant's size might trick a flea on its back. At *Kailua-Kena* the landscape is forgotten in a town rich in history. *Kamehameha the Great* ruled the islands from here until his death in 1819. *Kailua Pier* is home port for the sport fishing fleet and in the late afternoon the lucky anglers are photographed with their catches. Two good luncheon choices here: the *Paniolo Pizza* and the *Kona Galley* for fresh fish. For dinner: the S.S. *James Makee* is small and elegant.

Along the road through the Kona Coast lava fields graffiti takes a special form: short messages formed by placing pieces of white coral against the black lava. Bill loves Joan, Free Poland, or, top, the ancient symbol for Christ. In Kailua is the Hulihee Palace, *above left, the summer residence of Hawaiian chiefs and kings from 1837. Four miles south of Kailua is St. Peter's, the* Little Blue Church, *above right. In the gathering darkness, ancient wooden figures loom at Pu'uhonua o Honaunau, the City of Refuge National Historical Park. When Captain Cook came to Hawaii, there were laws of kamu of forbidden behavior. To be cleansed after committing a kamu a person went to a pu'uhonua (place of refuge) to be purified by a priest. Defeated warriors in tribal wars also could find refuge here.*

174

SPORTFISHING OFF KONA

The Hawaiian Islands, at the crossroads of game-fish migration routes, offer some of the most accessible, least expensive and best deep-sea fishing in the world. The southwest coast of Maui, the Waianae Coast of Oahu, and off Kauai's Na Pali cliffs are excellent locations. But the best is here, most especially for *the* game fish, Pacific Blue Marlin. (The largest ever caught on rod and reel is on display at the *International Market Place* in Waikiki, all 1,805 pounds of it.) June to November is the best period for blue marlin, but there's good fishing year-round. Also in these waters are black and striped marlin, *ahi* (yellow-fin tuna)

which can weigh 300 pounds, *mahimahi*, a dolphin-like fish that's a real fighter, *ono* (wahoo) which average 30 pounds, and *aku* (skipjack). Early in 1984, a record 1,656-pound, 16-foot 4-inch blue marlin was taken on Bart Miller's boat *Black Bart* by Gary Merriman of Atlanta, Georgia. Miller also holds the record for the most marlin taken in one day, one month and one year. The ultimate sports-fishing package: five days with Miller on the *Black Bart*, nights in a luxurious suite in the posh *Royal Seacliff*, and a Lincoln Continental to get from one to the other. Total cost: $5,000.

HILO

Although Hilo is the second-largest city in the islands and the county seat, it is a sleepy town. Its deep water harbor has made it the Big Island's port since 1778. One of the rainiest cities in the country, it averages 133 inches a year, and the humidity is usually high. The climate is perfect for growing orchids and anthuriums, and there are large fields of them south of the city. Jets from the mainland now fly directly to General Lyman Field here but most passengers head directly for the Kona Coast resorts. Hilo has attractions, though, for travelers if not for tourists. The old part of the city is fascinating, a combination of colonial waterfront and frontier town with a touch of seediness that would catch the fancy of a Graham Greene. There are old-time soda fountains that suggest *Andy Hardy* movies, Chinese shops where purchases still are run up on an aba-

cus, and thrift stores and swap shops. Except for *Banyan Drive*, Hilo's hotel row, and the *Liliuokalani Gardens*, there isn't a great deal to see. The *Lyman Mission and Museum* is an excellent example of life in that period of the island's history. Five minutes from downtown are the *Rainbow Falls* where the early morning sun usually produces spectacular rainbows, and *Onekahakaha Beach*, about three miles from Hilo on the south shore of the bay, is a nice place for a swim and a picnic. What gives Hilo its special character, however, is a sense of danger. It could be said that the city is between the devil and the deep blue sea. Hilo has been hit twice by giant tidal waves, or *tsunamis*: in 1868, killing 46 people; in 1946, killing some 170, 96 in Hilo alone. Lava from *Mauna Loa* also threatens the city. As this book went to press, Hilo still was on an evacuation alert from the 1984 eruption.

Looking back at Hilo from the gardens, opposite top left, it is hard to believe the gentle slope is Mauna Loa. A bridge in the gardens, opposite top right, is a good place to talk things over. A Japanese stone dragon looking properly fierce graces Liliuokalani Gardens, opposite center. A young resident of Hilo accompanies her mother on a leisurely stroll, opposite. A pond in the gardens, above, catches the late afternoon sun. Hilo gets much more rain than the arid Kona Coast.

NANILOA SURF

Banyan Drive, Hilo's hotel row, curves the north end of the bay lined with tall banyan trees, each named for a celebrity or dignitary who has visitied Hilo. The *Naniloa Surf* is the Queen of Banyan Drive, and it sits on the water's edge where black lava rocks meet the sea. Two ten-story wings contain 386 rooms (ask for a room with a view of the bay) and the best restaurant in Hilo, the *Sandalwood Room.* At dinner, the fresh fish is excellent, and the veal picatta is accompanied by the hotel's own pasta. For lunch, the *Banyan Broiler* does a nice job with pita bread sandwiches. There is a beautifully sited swimming pool, tennis, and a public golf course just across the street. And in a state known for the friendliness of its people, the staff here is exceptionally convivial. For orchid lovers, there are two special places nearby. The *Hilo Orchidarium* contains a wide variety of the beautiful flowers and it is an especially good place to photograph the blossoms. *Orchids of Hawaii* has a tour, a gift shop, and gives a corsage to every visitor. There are also *leis,* fresh cut flowers and Hawaiian dried foliage for sale.

Standing on a spur of land on Hilo Bay, the Naniloa Surf *catches the sea breeze and subtly lures its guests outdoors, top right. The hotel has the most attractive pool area of any in Hilo, a blessing on humid days. Right, a rear view of the "Queen of the Banyon Drive". Perhaps it's the moisture in the air, but for whatever reason the sunsets in Hilo are spectactular. When this picture, opposite, was taken in April 1984, one could turn around and see the red glow of the lava flow from Mauna Loa. The people of Hilo accept beauty and danger with equal equanimity.*

VOLCANO HOUSE

Perched on the rim of Kilauea and looking like a rustic lodge, *Volcano House* has 35 comfortable rooms and a great view of the crater from both the restaurant and the bar. Run by Sheraton for the National Park Service, this is one of several lodges that have been here since 1846. (Its most recent predecessor now is the nearby *Volcano Art Center*.) The food is good, although bus loads of tourists come for lunch. Reserve rooms in advance, particularly during an eruption.

VOLCANOES NATIONAL PARK

The focal point of the *Hawaii Volcanoes National Park* is the Kilauea Crater, opposite top, believed to be the current home of the mythological *Pele*, goddess of the volcanoes. She supposedly appears as a maiden or crone, depending on her whim, but always in a red dress just before an eruption, which she causes when angry. She must be short-tempered. Kilauea alone has erupted more than 30 times in the past 25 years. The crater is two-and-one-half miles long and two miles wide, comprising some 2,600 acres. It is 4,077 feet above sea level, 20,000 feet above the ocean floor. (Neighboring Mauna Loa is 13,677 feet above sea level, and 30,000 feet from the ocean floor, taller than Mount Everest. Another comparison: Mauna Loa's bulk is some 10,000 cubic miles; California's Mount Shasta is 80 cubic miles.) Even when Kilauea is not erupting, there are reminders that it is not at rest. Steam and sulphur vents, opposite below right, are everywhere in the crater and on the surrounding bluffs. A walk along Devastation Trail reveals a surrealistic landscape, below, with the whitened remains of trees here and there. Behind the tree remnant, left, is smoke rising from the 1984 eruption of Mauna Loa. Hardened lava is everywhere, bottom left. The park is interesting, weirdly beautiful, and most informative. The National Park Service has an excellent visitors center and smiling rangers are everywhere, below.

"The smell of sulphur is strong, but not unpleasant to the sinner."

Samuel Clemens on visiting the Kilauea Crater

Hot molten lava streams down the mountain from the spewing crater. This photograph and the one on pages 164–165 were taken from a helicopter at the 1984 eruption of Mauna Loa.

MISCELLANY

THE ISLANDS

Hawaii is a chain of eight islands, six of which are accessible to visitors. *Hawaii*, usually referred to as the *Big Island*, is known for its *Hawaii Volcanoes National Park*, black sand beaches, deep sea fishing, Kona coffee plantations, skiing on Mauna Loa, and macadamia nut farms. *Kauai* is noted for the rugged 3,000-foot-high Na Pali Cliffs, Waimea Canyon, an abundance of waterfalls, and Waialeale Crater, the wettest spot on earth. *Lanai*, one of the smallest Hawaiian islands, is the home of the world's largest pineapple plantation. Hunters visit for antelope, quail, partridge, wild goats, Axis deer and other species. *Maui* is ideal for skin diving, sailing, deep sea fishing, and whale-watching in season. Mount Haleakala, whose crater is large enough to hold Manhattan, is a major attraction. *Molokai* is considered by Hawaiians as the island where "paradise is the most intact." Lovely beaches are deserted and thickly forested mountains are accessible primarily to hikers. Skin diving, fishing and hunting are exceptional. The island is most closely associated with the former leper colony and the work there of Father Damien. *Oahu*, by far the most populous of the islands, is the site of Honolulu, Waikiki Beach, and Diamond Head. The windward side of the island offers spectacular soaring and surfing. The inaccessible islands are *Niihau* and *Kahoolawe*. *Niihau*, known as the "Forbidden Island," is privately owned and the home of several hundred pure-bred Hawaiians who speak Hawaiian fluently and live in isolation. Ranching is the major activity. The island is best known for Niihau shell *leis*; delicate, quite rare and expensive. *Kahoolawe* is the smallest of the eight major Hawaiian Islands and the only one that is uninhabited. The Navy has controlled the island since 1953 and uses it for bombing practice. It is only seven miles from *Maui*. Nighttime bombing practice sometimes resembles a firework display.

WEATHER

From April to October the weather in Hawaii is a balmy 73° to 88° farenheit. During the other months it is cooler and wetter, temperatures ranging from 65° to 90°. The temperature rarely rises above 90° or below 60°, except at higher altitudes. It can get quite chilly at Kalekala on *Maui*, Kokee on *Kauai*, and snow falls on Mauna Kea in the winter. Bring warm clothing if you plan to visit any of those areas. The Pacific and the northeasterly tradewinds are a natural air-conditioning system for the islands.

A CAPSULE HISTORY

300-500 A.D. Natives from the Marquesas Islands discover Hawaii and found settlements.

1100-1300 A.D. Tahitian settlers arrive and make slaves of the earlier inhabitants.

1400 A.D. The beginning of primitive Hawaiian culture.

1742 Captured Spanish map shows the Brit-

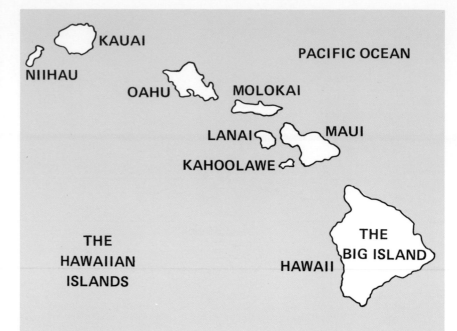

KAUAI

NIIHAU

PACIFIC OCEAN

OAHU MOLOKAI

LANAI MAUI

KAHOOLAWE

THE HAWAIIAN ISLANDS

THE BIG ISLAND

HAWAII

ish approximate location of the Hawaiian Islands.

January 17, 1778 Captain James Cook lands at *Kauai* and is mistaken for god Lono.

November 1778 Cook, having declared the Sandwich Islands (named for his patron the Earl of Sandwich) part of the British Empire, comes back and is treated like a returning god.

February 1779 Cook leaves again but a winter storm forces a return to Hawaii. The theft of a small boat touches off an incident in which Captain Cook is slain on February 13th. Before setting sail, the ships bombard native villages killing many innocent natives.

1786 British, French, Russian, Spanish and United States ships now stopping over in Hawaii.

1789 Kamehameha starts drive to unite the islands aided by Western cannon and advisors, notably British captain George Vancouver.

1794 Western ships discover Honolulu Harbòr. Kamehameha I defeats Kahekili at the battle of Ioa Needle and, having conquered *Maui*, invades *Oahu*.

1795 *Oahu* is conquered by Kamehameha I.

1810 All Hawaii is unified for the first time and Kamehameha I rules supreme.

1819 Death of Kamehameha I. His son Kiholiho ascends to the throne. When he proves a drunken weakling, Kamehameha's favorite wife Kaa'humanu takes control. Under her rule Christianity is introduced, the island order of forbidden practices, *kapu*, is broken, and a western form of parliamentary government is introduced.

April 4, 1820 Led by the Reverend Hiram Bingham, first group of Calvinists arrive from Boston.

1822 King George IV of Britain gives ship to Kamehameha II (Liholiho). The next

year he and his queen visit England and are royally entertained. Both die in England of measles.

May 1825 Kauikaeouli is crowned Kamehameha III.

1827 Catholic missionaries arrive but are driven out of Hawaii.

1830-1850 Plantations import for labor 180,000 Japanese, 125,000 Filipinos, 50,000 Chinese and 20,000 Portuguese.

1839 Catholic missionaries return under the protection of France. A Declaration of Civil Rights is written under the auspices of Kamehameha III.

1840 Whaling reaches peak. More than 500 ships visit yearly and the islands become dependent on the whale economy. Tension between missionaries and whalers mounts.

1848 Kamehameha II introduces the Great *Mahele* grants that provided one-third of the land each for the King, the government and the people. Two years later this was amended to permit white ownership of land for agricultural expansion.

1854 Alexander Liholiho becomes Kamehameha IV when hir heirless uncle dies. A United States move to annex the islands backfires when the new king visits the U.S. and is badly treated as a black.

1860 Hawaii now exporting 1.5 million pounds of sugar. Leprosy now becoming a problem in the islands.

1863 Kamehameha dies and his brother, Lot Liholiho, becomes Kamehameha V. The next year hè abolishes the 1854 Constitution, thus diminishing the power of the monarch and liberalizing the government.

1887 Kalalua overthrown by Reform Party.

1891 Kalalua dies in exile in California. Queen Liluokalani ascends to the throne.

186

office. Rivals for crown are the dowager Queen Emma, widow of Alexander Liholiho, and David Kalakaua. After her defeat her supporters riot.

1873 The white Reform Party forces acceptance of the Bayonnet Constitution which severely limits the power of the monarchy and strengthens the control of land owners.

1875 After two earlier failures a reciprocity treaty with the U.S. leads to the expansion of the sugar empire. The islands now are exporting nearly 20 million pounds of sugar a year.

1887 Kalakua overthrown by Reform Party.

1891 Kalahua dies in exile in California. Queen Liluokalani ascends to the throne.

July 7, 1897 U.S. Congress passes Joint Resolution of annexation. On August 12, 1898, Sanford B. Dole, acting as president of the Republic of Hawaii, hands the island nation over to U.S. Within hours troops arrive.

1900 Hawaii officially becomes a U.S. territory. (Most of the land in Hawaii is owned by the five percent white minority.)

1901 James D. Dole organizes the Hawaiian Pineapple Company.

1902 Transpacific cable completed between Honolulu and San Francisco.

1912 Duke Kamahamoku sets world swimming record at Olympics. (Hawaii now firmly under the economic control of the Big Five - the Doles, Thurstons, Alexanders, Baldwins and Cookes - and their power enabled them to appoint sympathetic governors and legislatures.)

1917 Liluokalani, the last ruling monarch, dies.

1924 Labor riot on sugar plantation results in 16 strikers dead, 101 arrested. Other participants in a later strike are killed by police on Kauai.

1935 Legalization of unions and collective bargaining in Hawaii.

December 7, 1941 Japanese airplanes attack Pearl Harbor killing 3,425 Americans. U.S. enters World War II the next day. Martial law is declared in Hawaii.

August 14, 1945 Victory over Japan Day ends World War II. (Japanese-Americans and Hawaiians distinguish themselves during war.)

1941-1946 Strikes help unions grow in power and replace the Big Five as the most potent force in Hawaii.

1946 Huge tidal wave (taunami) devastates Hilo and kills 150 islanders.

1946 Hawaiian Visitor's Bureau formed to promote tourism.

August 24, 1969 Hawaii becomes 50th state. (First jet plane service to Hawaii sends tourism booming.) The same year Astronauts in Apollo's successful lunar landing return to earth at Hawaii.

1974 George R. Ariyoshi becomes first Japanese-American to be elected governor of any state.

1977 Tourists now outnumber residents by

four to one.

1983 Hawaii's population reaches one million.

1984 Hawaii celebrates 25th Anniversary of Statehood.

CALENDAR OF EVENTS

There's something going on in Hawaii practically every day of the year. The islands have no seasons and special events abound. Following is a list of events that occur *every* year. (For a comprehensive list for the period of your holiday write the Hawaii Visitors Bureau nearest you.)

JANUARY—*Hulu Bowl Game* at Aloha Stadium, Honolulu. *Narcissus Festival* celebrates the Chinese New Year in Honolulu's Chinatown. *Opening of State Legislature*—Legislative session begins with speeches, Hawaiian music and hula dancing.

FEBRUARY—*Hawaiian Open International Golf Tournament* at Waialae Golf and Country Club, Honolulu. *Great Waikoloa Horse Races and Rodeo* in Waikoloa on the Big Island. *Mauna Kea Ski Meet. Cherry Blossom Festival*, Honolulu.

MARCH—*Japanese Girl's Day* at the University of Hawaii, Honolulu. *St. Patrick's Day Parade*, Waikiki.

APRIL—*Buddha Day*, various festivals on various islands. *Hawaiian Festival of Music*, Honolulu. *Punchbowl Easter Sunrise Service*, Honolulu, *Merrie Monarch Festival*, various locations.

MAY—*Lei Day* on which *everyone* wears a *lei*, with special events at Waikiki Shell, Kapiolani Park, Honolulu.

JUNE—*50th State Fair* at Aloha Stadium, Honolulu. *Miss Hawaii Pageant*, Blaisdell Center, Honolulu. *Mission Houses Museum Fancy Fair*, Honolulu. *Annual Hawaiian Festival of Music*, Waikiki Shell.

JULY—*Hilo Orchid Society Flower Show. Makawao, Naalehu* and *Parker Ranch Rodeos* on *Maui* and the Big Island. *International Festival of the Pacific* celebrating the

Big Island's varied ethnic heritage, Hilo.

AUGUST—*Obon Odori Festival*, the Buddhist Festival of Souls, observed on *Oahu* with a paper lantern ceremony. *Macadamia Nut Augustfest* celebrates the harvest on the Big Island.

SEPTEMBER—*Waikiki Annual Rough Water Swim, Hawaii County Fair.* Aloha Festival, a week of festivities in all the islands, including the famous 27½ mile canoe race from *Molokai* to *Oahu.*

OCTOBER—*Maui County Fair. Annual Orchid Plant & Flower Show*, Blaisdell Center, Honolulu.

NOVEMBER—*Ne Mele O Maui*, Lahaina festival with luaus, arts and crafts, music and dance. *Annual Michelob Polo Cup and Bar-B-Que*, Makawao, *Maui. Christmas Fair* is an open craft market with an emphasis on Christmas items, Mission Houses Museum, Honolulu.

DECEMBER—*Hawaiian Pro Surfing Championships*, Banzai Pipeline, North Shore, *Oahu. Festival of Trees*, a decorated Christmas tree exhibit, Blaisdell Center, Honolulu. *Annual Honolulu Marathon*, beginning at Aloha Tower and ending at Kapiolani Park, Honolulu. *Pearl Harbor Day*, special service at the USS Arizona Memorial. *Bodhi Day*, ceremonies at Buddhist temples mark the Japanese Day of Enlightment.

VISITORS BUREAU

The *Hawaii Visitors Bureau* is an excellent source of free information on Hawaii. The main office is at 2270 Kalakaua Ave., Honolulu 86815, and there are branches at 441 Lexington Ave., New York 10017; 180 North Michigan Ave., Chicago 60601; 209 Post St., San Francisco 94108; and 3440 Wilshire Blvd., Los Angeles 90010.

STATE BIRD, FLOWER, TREE, ETC.

Hawaii's state bird is the *nene* (pronounced nay-nay), a variety of goose. The *nene* was almost extinct in 1949 when they became protected by law and a restoration project was established. There are now several hundred wild *nene* and birds are being raised in captivity to join them. The state flower is the hibiscus which is grown everywhere in the islands. There are more than 5,000 varieties of hibiscus that come in a rainbow of colors and combinations. In addition, each island has its own official flower: *Hawaii Island*, Red Lehua, (Ohia); *Maui*, Lokelani (Pink Cottage Rose); *Molokai*, White Kukui Blossom; *Kahoolawe*, Hinahina (Beach Heliotrope); *Lanai, Ilima, Kauai,* Mokihana (Green Berry), and *Niihau,* White Pupu Shell. The state tree is the indigenous *kukui,* better known as the candlenut. The nuts of the *kukui* provided the ancient Hawaiians with light, oil, relishes and medicants. The state marine mammal is the humpback whale. The last session of Territorial Legislature on April 23, 1959, designated "The Aloha State" as the official nickname for the State of Hawaii. The state flag has eight stripes of red, white, and blue. The field is a variation of the British Union Jack, not because Britian once ruled Hawaii—it didn't, but the Hawaiian who commissioned the flag liked the looks of the Union Jack.

THE PEOPLE

Caucasians, called *haoles* locally, make up 29 percent of Hawaii's population. Not all are descendants of missionaries or retired servicemen. Included are European planters, Portuguese cowboys and South American laborers. Actually, the largest ethnic group, strictly speaking, is *Japanese,* accounting for a bit more than 25 percent. *Hawaiians,* the descendants, wholly or in part, of the Polynesians, represent 20 percent. Other major ethnic groups are *Filipinos, Chinese, Koreans* and a growing number of *Samoans.*

THE HAWAIIAN LANGUAGE

Hawaii is the only state that has two official languages, English and Hawaiian. A Polynesian dialect, Hawaiian is one of the world's most melodious. It consists of only 12 letters: the vowels *a, e, i, o, u,* and the consonants *h, k, l, m, n, p,* and *w,* and is the shortest alphabet of any language in the world. Anyone familiar with Spanish should have no trouble with Hawaiian vowels. They almost always are pronounced as follows: a like *a* in far; e like *e* in bed; i like *ee* in see; o like *o* in sole, and u like *oo* in moon. It is extremely rare for a visitor to hear someone using Hawaiian in ordinary conversation, but many Hawaiian words and phrases pop up in English sentences, and there are thousands of Hawaiian songs sung in Hawaiian. (*Kawaiahao Church* in Honolulu has sermons in Hawaiian.) There has been increasing interest in the language as a result of a native cultural renaissance, but it hasn't seemed to have had any affect, as yet. Two other curiosities of the language should be noted. There is a glottal stop (') that works as sort of an eighth consonant. It's pronounced, or rather not pronounced, as the pause in "oh-oh" is (or is not) pronounced. Also there is a certain amount of confusion about the consonant "w". When it's the first letter of a word it's pronounced as "w" (Waikiki, for instance) but when it follows *e* or *i* the "w" is pronounced as if it were a "v" (Ewa is pronounced Eva.) Which doesn't explain why most Hawaiians pronounce the name of their state as if it has a "v" in it.'

WORDS AND PHRASES

aikane - friend *(eye-kah-nay)*
akamai - wise, smart *(ah-kah-mye)*
alii - chief *(ah-lee-ee)*
aloha - hello, goodbye, love *(ah-loh-ha}*
hale - house *(hah-lay)*
hono - bay *(hon-noh)*
huhu - angry *(hoo-hoo)*
huki - pull *(hoo-kee)*
huli - turn *(hoo-lee)*
imu - underground oven *(ee-moo)*
kai - ocean, salt water *(kye)*
kala - money *(kah-la)*
kamaaina -oldtimer *(kah-mah-eye-nah)*
kane -man *(kah-nay)*
pkapu - forbidden *(kah-poo)*
kaukau food *(kow-kow)*
keiki - child *(kay-ee-kee)*
kokua - help *(koh-koo-ah)*
lanai -porch, patio *(lah-nah-ee)*
lei - garland *(lav-ee)*
luau - feast *(loo-ah-oo)*
mahalo - thank you *(mah-hah-lo)*
makai - toward the sea *(mah-kah-ee)*
malihini - newcomer *(mah-lee-hee-nee)*
mauka - toward the mountains *(mah-oo-kah)*
mauna - mountain *(mah-na)*
moana - ocean *(moh-ah-na)*
muumuu -loose-fitting long dress *(moo-moo)*
nui - big *(noo-ee)*
ono - delicious *(oh-noh)*

pali - cliff *(pah-lee)*
paniolo - cowboy *(pah-nee-oh-loh)*
pau - finished *(pah-oo)*
pua - flower *(poo-ah)*
puka - hole *(poo-kah)*
pupu - hors d'oeuvre *(poo-poo)*
tutu - grandmother *(too-too)*
wahine - woman *(wah-hee-nay)*
wai - fresh water *(wah-ee)*
wiki wiki - quickly, hurry *(wee-kee wee-kee)*
Aloha nui loa - much love *(ah-loh-hah noo-ee loh-ah)*
Hauoli la Hanau - happy birthday *(hah-oo oh-le lan hah-nah-oo)*
Hauoli Makahiki Hou - Happy New Year *(hah-oo-oh-lee mah-kah-hee-kee hoh-oo)*
Komo mai - come in *(koh-moh- mah-ee)*
Meme Kalikimaka - Merry Christmas *(may-may kah-lee-kee-mah-kah)*
Okole maluna - Bottoms up, cheers *(oh koh-lee mah-loo-na)*

SOME ISLAND DISHES

chicken luau—chicken simmered slowly with taro leaves and coconut milk.
haupia—a sweet white pudding made from coconut cream and arrowroot.
kim chi—highly spiced pickled vegetables (Korean).
laulau—pork, butterfish, and taros wrapped in fresh ti leaves and steamed.
lomilomi—salt salmon shredded and mixed with chopped green onions, tomatoes and crushed ice.
malasadas—sugared doughnuts without holes that are eaten hot (Portuguese).
manapua—a steamed bun filled with sweet roasted pork, called dim sum everywhere but Hawaii.
pui—the most Hawaiian of dishes, a gunmetal-colored, slightly sour replacement for potatoes in the island diet. Made from mashed taro root.
saimin—noodles cooked in a chicken or shrimp broth. Considered "fast food" in Hawaii.
sashimi—thinly sliced raw fish served with a hot sauce (Japanese)
shave ice—a paper cone filled with finely shaved ice and flavored with various syrups.
sushi—small patties of rice mixed with mirin vinegar around bits of pickled vegetables or fish. (Japanese)
tempura—shellfish, fish or vegetables dipped in a light batter and deep fried (Japanese).
teriyaki— strips of beef marinated in a sauce of ginger, sugar and soy sauce (Japanese).

FLYING TO HAWAII

United Air Lines has been flying to Hawaii since 1947 and no airline links more mainland gateway cities to Hawaii. Some seasons the airline carries as much as one-half of the Hawaii-bound traffic. Other U.S. airlines servicing Hawaii include *American, Continental, Northwest Orient, Pan American, Western* and *World.*

AROUND THE ISLANDS

Aloha Airlines flies full-size jets to all the islands except Lanai. *Mid-Pacific* flies 60-passenger prop jets to Lanai. An alternative way to island hop is by the small planes of *Royal Hawaiian Air Service,* which has daily schedules to ten island airports. The pilots go out of their way to make sure the passengers enjoy the scenery.

CAR RENTALS

The best way to enjoy any of the islands is by car and, happily, the rates in Hawaii are among the least expensive in the country. All the major rent-a-car companies—*Hertz, Avis, Budget, Dollar, Gray Line, American International Thrifty* and *National*—are represented and their rates are competitive with local companies. Two tips: be sure you have a reservation *before* you go to any of the islands, and take the unlimited-mileage cars.

SAILBOAT CHARTERS

Hawaiiana Yacht Charters has a bareboat charter fleet, most in the 30- to 40-foot class, that are available for short cruises off Oahu or for inter-island tours. The firm also operates the *Hawaii Sailing Academy* with courses for sailors of all ability levels. *Seabern Yachts,* Lahaina, Maui, has charter craft from 24 to 29 feet. *Lanai Sea Charters* has a 35-foot sloop, *Stacked Deck,* that is available for a variety of charter arrangements. Note: the best sailing is in the waters between Lanai, Maui and Molokai.

A GOLFER'S HAWAII

Besides the resort courses previously described, there are a number of courses in the islands open to the public. This listing includes the name, location, length, weekday and weekend rates, and the cost of a cart if it is not included. If the course is at a resort the rate for non-guests is given. Rates are subject to change and are included only for the purpose of comparison.

OAHU

Ala Wai Golf Course, Honolulu. 6,474; $2.50; $4; $10.40

Bay View Golf Center, Kaneohe. 2,231 (Par 54); $4; $5; pull cart only, $.75

Hawaii Country Club, Wanilawa. 5,601; $12; $17; cart inc.

Hawaii Kai Championship, Honolulu. 6,350; $20.80; $23.92; cart inc.

Hawaii Kai Executive, Honolulu. 2,542 (Par 56); $6.24; $7.80; $7.28

Hyatt Kullima Resort, Kahuku. 4,126; $26; $26; cart inc.

Kahuku Golf Course, Kahuku. 2,725 (9 holes, par 35); $1.50; $2; $.50

Mahaka Valley Country Club, Waianae. 6,748; $14.56; $17.60; cart inc.

Millani Golf Course, Millani Town. 6,360; $14.50; $18.50; cart inc.

Moanalua Golf Club, Honolulu. 3,042 (9 holes, par 36; $14.50; $18; cart inc.

Olomana Golf Links, Waimanalo. 6,321; $14.50; $18; cart inc.

Pali Golf Course, Kaneohe. 6,493; $2.50; $4; $10.40.

Pearl Country Club, Aiea. 6,491; $20-16 (rates change at 1:30 PM); $25-20; cart inc.

Ted Makalena Golf Course, Waipahu. 5,756; $2.50; $4; $10.40

KAUAI

Kauai Surf Golf & Country Club, Kalapaki Beach. 6,808; $18; $18; $7 (per person).

Kukuiolono Golf Course, Kalaheo. 3,806 (9 holes, par 35) $5; $5; $5 ($7 weekends)

Wailua Golf Course, Wailua. 6,665; $7; $8; $9.36.

MAUI

Makena Golf Club, Kihei. 6,798; $18; $18; $8

Maui Country Club, Paia (Visitors Monday only; separate charge front and back nine, each $7; $6; $6).

Pukalani Country Club, Pukalani. (Separate charges, front nine: $4; $4; $6; back nine: $7; $6; $6).

Royal Kaanapali North, Kaanapali. 7,179; $23; $23; $10

Royal Kaanapali South, Kaanapali. 6,758; $23; $23; $10

Waiehu Municipal Golf Course, Waiehu. 6,367; $10; $15; $10.40

MOLOKAI

Ironwood Hills Golf Course, Kualapuu. 2,750 (9 holes, par 35) $5; $5; no carts

Kaluakoi Golf Coourse, Maunaloa. 6,211; $16; $16; $8

LANAI

Cavandish Golf Course, Lanai. 3,100 (9 holes, par 36) $5; $5; no carts.

HAWAII

Banyan Golf Center, Hilo. 2,745 (9 holes, par 35); $3; $3; $4

Hamakua Country Club, Honokaa.

2,205 (9 holes; par 33) $3; $3; no carts.

Hilo Municipal Golf Course, Hilo. 5,991; $3; $4; $10

Keauhou-Kona Country Club, Keauhou-Kona. 6,800; $21; $21; $16

Seamountain Golf Course, Punaluu. 6,108; $14; $14; $14.

Volcano Golf & Country Club, Volcano. 6,119; $14; $14; $12

Waikoloa Beach Golf Course, South Kohala. 6,645; $20; $20; $15

Waikoloa Village Golf Course, Waikoloa. 6,316; $20; $20; $15

NUDE BEACHES

There are nude beaches on most of the islands although they are more the province of young *haoles* and visitors than the native Hawaiians, who seem to have forgotten that they're the ones who probably started it all. Since 1979 the law is that toplessness is legal in secluded sites among consenting people. Full nudity is tolerated in some areas and leads to arrest in others. The beaches here should pose no problem providing a reasonable amount of discretion is used. (It should go without saying that you will not be welcomed if you come only to gawk or, particularly, to take photographs.)

OAHU—Near the lighthouse at the foot of Diamond Head there is an access road with a steep walkway nearby leading to the beach. Weekdays are better than weekends when the beach usually is patrolled. KAUAI—*Kalalau Beach* on the Na Pali Coast is a beautiful nude beach, particularly in the summer when the surf is calmer. It's an 11-mile hike from Haena but also is reachable by Zodiac boats for day trips. *Polihale State Park* on the southwest tip of Kauai attracts nudists. Walk south for 20 minutes after you reach the beach. MAUI—One mile past the Inter-Continental Maui in the Wailea area is Polo Beach. Another three miles down the dirt road is a turn in to Big Makena Beach. Walk west to *Little Makena Beach* for full nudity. Fifteen miles beyond Hana is the *Haleakala National Park* where nudists swim in the upper pools of the *Seven Sacred Pools.* HAWAII—About five miles south of the airport on the Kona Coast is Honokohau Harbor Road. Drive to the right of the harbor and take the gravel road to *Honokohau Beach.*

MARIJUANA

One of the larger cash crops in Hawaii is cannabis and the connoisseurs have high praise for *Kona Gold* and *Maui Powie.* The laws here are as strict as anywhere else in the country, though, and so is the enforcement of them. It would be a shame to spoil a holiday by being busted.

HAIL MAUI
FULL OF GRASS

HOTELS & RESORTS

HAWAII

Kona Village Resort, P.O. Box 1299, Kailua-Kona, HI 96740, Phone: (808) 325-5555; 81 individual Polynesian cottages on the beach, pool, tennis courts; Full American Plan; very expensive.

Mauna Kea Beach Hotel, P.O. Box 218, Kamuela, HI 96743; Phone: (808) 882-7222; 310 rooms on the beach; pool, golf course, tennis courts; Modified American Plan; very expensive.

Mauna Lani Bay Hotel, P.O. Box 4000, Kawaihae, HI 96743; Phone: (808) 885-6622, toll free (800) 367-2323; 351 rooms on the beach; pool, tennis courts, golf course, health club; European Plan; very expensive.

Naniloa Surf, 93 Banyan Dr., Hilo, HI 96720; Phone: (808) 935-0831, toll free (800) 367-2323; 351 rooms on Hilo bay; Swimming pool, tennis courts; European Plan; moderate to expensive.

Volcano House, Hawaii Volcanoes National Park, HI 96718; Phone: (808) 967-7391, toll free (800) 325-3535; 37 rooms on the edge of the Kilauea Crater; European Plan; Inexpensive.

KAUAI

Coco Palms Hotel, P.O. Box 1005, Lihue, Kauai,HI 96766; Phone: (808) 822-4921, toll free (800) 277-4700; 416 rooms across the street from the beach; pool, tennis courts, European Plan, moderate.

Kiahuna Plantation, R.R. 1, Box 73, Koloa, Kauai, HI 96756; phone: (808) 742-6411, toll free (800) 367-5360; 333 condominium apartments on or near the beach; pool, golf course, tennis courts; housekeeping apartments with restaurants on grounds, moderate to expensive.

Kokee Lodge, P.O. Box 518, Kekaha, Kauai, HI 96752; phone: (808) 335-6061; 12 one- and two-bedroom cabins in state park (no maid service); restaurant nearby; inexpensive.

Princeville Condominiums, (Information: *Makai Club Cottages* or *Pali Ke Kua*, c/o Paradise Management Corp., Kukui Plaza C-207, 50 S. Beretania St., Honolulu, HI 96813; phone: (808) 538-7145, toll free (800) 367-7090); housekeeping condominium apartments near beach on 27-hole golf course; pools; restaurants on grounds, expensive.

Sheraton Coconut Beach Hotel, Coconut Plantation, Kapaa, Kauai, HI 96746; phone: (808) 822-3455, toll free (800) 344-8484; 311 rooms on the beach; pool, tennis courts; European Plan, moderate to expensive.

The Waiohai, R.R. 1, P.O. Box 174, Poipu Beach, Kauai, HI 96758; phone: (808) 277-4700, toll free (800) 277-4700; 460 rooms on the beach; pool, tennis courts, golf course; European Plan, expensive.

OAHU

Halekulani Hotel, 2199 Kalia Rd., Honolulu, HI 95815; phone: (808) 923-2311, toll free (800) 626-2626; 456 rooms and suites on Waikiki Beach; pool; European Plan; expensive.

Hyatt Regency Waikiki, 2424 Kalakaua Ave., Honolulu, HI 96815; phone: (808) 922-9292, toll free (800) 228-9000; 1,234 rooms across the street from the beach; pool; European Plan; moderate to expensive.

Ilikai, 1777 Ala Moana Dr., Honolulu, HI 96815; phone: (808) 949-3811, toll free (800) 228-1212; 800 rooms on beach lagoon; pools, tennis complex; European Plan, moderate.

John Guild Inn, 2001 Vancouver Drive, Honolulu, HI 96822; phone: (808) 947-6019; period guest rooms in restored mansion in Manoa Valley; continental breakfast included in rates; expensive.

Kahala Hilton, 5000 Kahala Ave., Honolulu, HI 96816; phone (808) 734-2211; 370 rooms and suites on the beach; pool, European Plan, very expensive.

Moana Hotel, 2365 Kalakaua Ave., Honolulu, HI 96815; phone: (808) 922-3111, toll free (800) 325-3535; 387 rooms in historic hotel on Waikiki Beach; European Plan, inexpensive to moderate.

Royal Hawaiian Hotel, 2259 Kalakaua Ave., Honolulu, HI 96815; phone: (808) 923-7311, toll free (800) 325-3535; 569 rooms on the beach; pool; European Plan; expensive.

Sheraton Makaha Resort and Country Club, P.O. Box 896, Waianae, Oahu, HI 96792; phone: (808) 695-9511, toll free (800) 334-8484; 196 rooms in valley; golf course, pool, tennis courts; European Plan, moderate.

MAUI

Heavenly Hana Inn, Hana, Maui, HI 96713; phone: (808) 248-8442; eight rooms in Japanese-style inn; no food served; inexpensive.

Hotel Hana-Maui, P.O. Box 8, Hana, Maui, HI 96713; phone: 248-8211; 61 rooms; swimming pool; beach facilities nearby, tennis courts; Full American Plan, expensive.

Hyatt Regency Mauii, Kaanapali Beach Resort, Kaanapali, Maui, HI 96761; phone: (808) 667-7474, toll free (800) 228-9000; 815 rooms on beach; pool, tennis courts, European Plan; expensive to very expensive.

Hotel Inter-Continental, P.O. Box 779, Kihei, Maui, HI 96753; phone: (808) 879-1922, toll free (800) 367-2960; 600 rooms on the beach at Wailea; pool, golf course, tennis courts; European Plan; expensive.

Kapalua Bay Hotel & Villas, One Bay Drive, Kapalua, Maui, HI 96761; phone: (808) 669-5656, toll free (800) 545-4000; 196 rooms on the beach; pool, golf course, tennis courts; Modified American Plan optional, very expensive.

Pioneer Inn, 658 Wharf St., Lahaina, Maui, HI 96761; phone: 661-3636; 48 rooms in historic hotel on Lahaina Harbor; pool; inexpensive.

Stouffer's Wailea Beach, Wailea, Maui, HI 96753; Phone 879-4900; 350 rooms on the beach; pool, golf course, tennis courts; very expensive.

LANAI

Hotel Lanai, P.O. Box A-119, Lanai, HI 96763; phone: (808) 565-6605; ten rooms in former sugar plantation guest house overlooking town; tennis courts and nine-hole golf course nearby; European Plan, inexpensive.

MOLOKAI

Sheraton Molokai Hotel, P.O. Box 1977, Maunaloa, Molokai, HI 96770; phone: (808) 325-3535, toll free (800) 325-3535; 292 rooms in thatched-roof cottages on the beach; pool, golf course, tennis courts; expensive.

INDEX